D1567824

THE AGENTRY AGENDA™:

Selling **FOOD** in a
Frictionless Marketplace

Are You Ready?

Glen A. Terbeek

In recognition of the importance of preserving the written word, The American Book Company has a policy to print books of value in the United States on acid-free paper and we exert our best commitment to that end.

Copyright © Glen A. Terbeek
Published by Breakaway Strategies, Inc.

All Rights Reserved. No part of this book may be reproduced in whole or in part in any form whatsoever without written permission of the publisher or the author. Requests for permission or further information should be addressed to the Permissions Department, The American Book Company.

Library of Congress Cataloging-in-Publication Data

Terbeek, Glen A.-1942
The **AGENTRY AGENDA**™: Selling Food in a Frictionless Marketplace
No index
ISBN 1-928948-00-6
1. Case Studies. 2. Consumers. 3. E-commerce. 4. Food Industry.
5. Marketing. 6. Profitability. 7. Relationship marketing. 8. Strategy. 9. Title

MANAGING EDITOR: Don J. Beville

EDITOR: Maggie Hoag

TEXT AND COVER DESIGN: Designer's Ink

CARTOONS: Marshall Clark of Norwood, Ohio

PRINTED in the United States of American by
The American Book Company
7105 Winding Creek Lane, Lower Level
Chesterfield, Va. 23832 (804-276-3201)

For information on ordering this title please contact our Web Site at:
www.**AgentryAgenda**.com

10 9 8 7 6 5 4 3 2 1

> **Dedication** To Judy, my devoted wife, best friend, and astute advisor who supported me over the 33 years of my career. I love you. To Todd and Mark, my wonderful sons. I'm so proud of you. To my father for teaching me the values I cherish and for advising me to "do what you enjoy." I miss you. And to my Mom, thanks for so much, I love you.

I would like to thank the following people for helping me throughout my career.

Acknowledgements

- All those who have worked at SMART STORE over the years and believed in thought leadership, especially John Hollis, Kent Brooks, Fred Schneider, Mike Gorshe, Kevin Duffill, David Symonds, and Renee Sang.

- My partners and others in the Food and Consumer Goods Industry program at Andersen Consulting, for supporting SMART STORE™.

- Vic Orler, for conducting several of the difficult-to-do industry wide studies that were so valuable in defining the **AGENTRY AGENDA**™.

- Bob Grottke, for his friendship, his enthusiasm for the industry, and his mentoring over the years.

- John Strang, for teaching me that work can be fun.

- Mike O'Connor, for his friendship and supportive, strategic counsel over the last 20 years.

- All my industry friends from around the world, for being a source of encouragement and valuable ideas.

- Maggie Hoag, my writer over the years who was able to interpret my frequently jumbled thoughts and made them so understandable.

- Marshall Clark, the very creative cartoonist who helped to make this book enjoyable to read.

- Jo-Lynn Marshall, my friend and assistant who kept me organized and on track, no matter where I was in the world.

- Melva Gage, for her friendship, research, editing help, and dedication over 30 years.

- The professors at Hope College, for teaching me to ask questions.

agent: (ā ′jent) 1) One with the power or authority to act. 2) A means or mode by which something is done or caused. 3) **A retailer that has earned the right to anticipate and deliver goods and services which fulfill the needs and expectations of individual shoppers, whether through a virtual or actual store, because of relationships built on trust.**

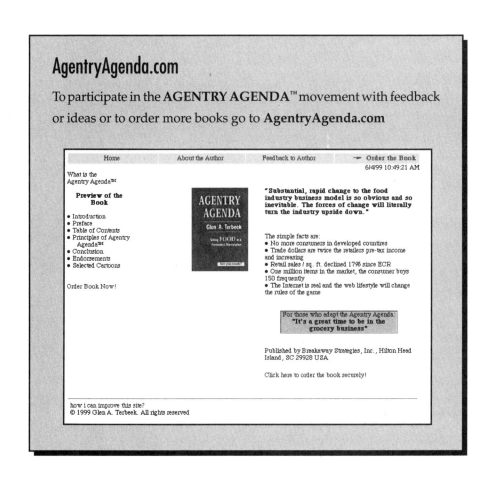

AgentryAgenda.com

To participate in the **AGENTRY AGENDA**™ movement with feedback or ideas or to order more books go to **AgentryAgenda.com**

| Home | About the Author | Feedback to Author | → Order the Book |

6/4/99 10:49:21 AM

What is the
Agentry Agenda™

**Preview of the
Book**

● Introduction
● Preface
● Table of Contents
● Principles of Agentry
   Agenda™
● Conclusion
● Endorsements
● Selected Cartoons

Order Book Now!

AGENTRY
AGENDA
Glen A. Terbeek
Selling FOOD in a
Frictionless Marketplace

"Substantial, rapid change to the food industry business model is so obvious and so inevitable. The forces of change will literally turn the industry upside down."

The simple facts are:
● No more consumers in developed countires
● Trade dollars are twice the retailers pre-tax income and increasing
● Retail sales / sq. ft. declined 17% since ECR
● One million items in the market, the consumer buys 150 frequently
● The Internet is real and the web lifestyle will change the rules of the game

For those who adapt the Agentry Agenda:
"It's a great time to be in the grocery business"

Published by Breakaway Strategies, Inc., Hilton Head Island, SC 29928 USA

Click here to order the book securely!

how i can improve this site?
© 1999 Glen A. Terbeek. All rights reserved

> hen I started SMART STORE ™ in 1988, the name SMART stood for *Super Marketing through Applied Retail Technology*. Even then, the seeds of change were starting to break ground. The message of SMART STORE™ was twofold: retailers and manufacturers needed a new understanding of the power of marketing *done right*; and technology would both drive and enable this new understanding, while transforming how retailers and manufacturers thought about their businesses. Now, those seeds of change are flowering into nothing less than a new model for the industry. *It's a great time to be in the grocery business!*

"This vital book comes at a critical time in the food industry's history. While not everyone will welcome the conclusions and recommendations contained here, the book is a wake up call to the industry and represents an opportunity for the industry to remake itself for the benefits of those it serves and itself. We may well look back at this book as being the catalyst that began a remaking of the food distribution industry. It is absolutely a must read!"

WILLIAM J. BRODBECK
President, Relationship Marketing,
Retired President & CEO, Brodbeck Enterprises
Dick's Supermarkets

"A future business model for the food industry: how supermarkets and suppliers will align in a new marketplace in which e-commerce and traditional retailing will combine to create new value for the customer; a book that was waiting to be written."

DENISE LARKING COSTE
Former Executive Vice President, CIES Food Business Forum

"Glen Terbeek has been and still is an important factor in the grocery business. He is a creative iconoclast of the first order. Some of his partners at Andersen Consulting thought he was mad when he created SMART STORE™ to research the future issues of the industry. To add to their concerns, he used an unoccupied chemical laboratory belonging to Northwest-

ern University. From there he moved to a hundred-year-old loft building in a "questionable" neighborhood in Chicago. But SMART STORE™ was such a good idea it rose above it humble surroundings to locations in London, Sydney, and Tokyo as well. Senior executives of almost every company in the industry have visited SMART STORE™. Many several times.

You will find this book as challenging and as imaginative as that first version of SMART STORE™. It will make you think. You may disagree, that's okay with Glen. In any event it will stimulate your mind and challenge your status quo. We all need that from time to time."

MIKE O'CONNOR
Professor, Writer, and Senior Consultant

"This book will be useful to any executive who is not content to drift with the industry. Today the industry thrashes around because it does not have a clear vision of where it is going. Without knowing where the industry is going, any executive can see any road — ECR, loyalty programs, consolidation—as one that will take them into an undefined future. With this book in hand, an executive can plot a course that can take them from where they are today to the world of the Frictionless Marketplace and **AGENTRY** Marketing. I look forward to seeing the book in print and doing its work. I see this book as a labor of love in which Glen gives back to the industry the support it gave to him."

LEO SHAPIRO, PhD
Founder, Leo Shapiro and Associates, Inc.

"The food industry is in the midst of an era of cost-cutting and consolidation in response to a white-hot competitive and mature food industry. Yet the industry continues to struggle to create profitable growth. All companies are requiring fresh, breakaway strategies to survive in the New Millennium. With **AGENTRY AGENDA**™, Glen Terbeek continues his renowned championing for progressive change in the industry. The **AGENTRY AGENDA**™ is a brilliantly strategic new industry model where all will win; consumers, manufacturers and retailers. He has delivered a "just in time" gem. It is a "must read" for food industry executives; and required reading for my students in Food Marketing Management."

JOHN W. ALLEN, PhD
Professor of Food Marketing
Director, Food Industry Alliance
Michigan State Unniversity

"Glen Terbeek has written a must read book for everyone involved with the strategies of the food retailing business. Glen does a superb job of outlining the sequential logic which brought us to where we are today and presents a compelling case as to why major changes must take place to create a viable future. A future where everyone can win, the manufacture, the retailer and especially the consumer. The **AGENTRY AGENDA**™ will challenge your thinking. Read it."

Thomas W. Vadeboncoeur
Retired Vice President Customer Marketing, Coca-Cola
Greater Europe
CEO Goodheart Resource, consulting

"This is a book about a revolution. It challenges the most basic premise of the current retailing practices (particularly supermarket retailing)- the notion that mass marketing is efficient, good and necessary. In its place genuinely new and exciting premises are proposed; The Frictionless Marketplace and The **AGENTRY AGENDA**™.

The Internet is discussed as an every day part of the daily life of most consumers in the future, and talks to the changes in how they shop, and also the responses that the retailers need to create. A bombshell: how the realities of brick and mortar retailing are at risk in the future. There are so many ideas and examples in the book I found myself writing notes in the margin of every page.

I think retailers, and manufacturers too, will find the book inspiring. What it proposes is developing the ability to serve the exact needs of the consumers one at a time, when and where, needed. And doing it at a lower cost.

This is a book to live with, not just to buy and read on airplanes. There is so much that gets your creative juices flowing."

Norman H. McMillan
Partner, McMillan-Doolittle

Glen Terbeek's recently retired from Andersen Consulting where his consulting career spanned over 33 years. Mr. Terbeek focused almost exclusively in the food industry, serving companies in the United States, Europe, South America and the Pacific Basin. He served as a personal advisor to several manufacturer and retail CEO's in the US, UK, Continental Europe and Japan.

While serving as the Managing Partner of Andersen Consulting's Food and Packaged Goods Industry Practice, Mr. Terbeek spearheaded the development of Andersen Consulting's research and development center, SMART STORE™, established in 1989. Its mission was to study the global issues and changes facing the food and packaged goods industry through locations in Chicago, London, Sydney and Tokyo.

He addresses a number of industry conferences every year in Europe, Latin America, Asia and the US, speaking on a wide variety of topics ranging from technology and finance to marketing and logistics issues facing the food industry. Among the industry conferences at which Mr. Terbeek has been a speaker are the Food Marketing Institute (FMI), Council of Logistics Management, Grocery Manufacturers of America, Inc. (GMA) and CIES, the Food Business Forum. He has lectured at the University of Chicago, Graduate School of Business; Harvard University, Graduate School of Business; and the Peter E. Drucker Graduate Management Center. He is considered a futurist by many who know him.

Mr. Terbeek received his M.B.A. in quantitative methods from the University of Michigan and his B.A. from Hope College.

Ten years ago, SMART STORE™ [1] opened as a research center where industry leaders could discuss new ideas for improving the overall performance of the food industry. Then, the SMART STORE™ concern was that *new* technologies were being applied to *old* ways of doing business. PC-based applications addressed labor scheduling, or Direct Store Delivery (DSD), or warehouse management, or space management. But what was helping the store manager do a better job of satisfying the needs of local shoppers? Nothing. What was helping the retailer distinguish the value it delivered in a crowded marketplace? Nothing. At the very least, what was helping retailers drive down operating costs in an effort to keep a grip on ever-slipping margins? Nothing. The problem was not technology; the problem was trading practices better suited to a time when the industry was young.

In the first few years of SMART STORE™, research pointed to new trading practices — *new ways of doing business* — enabled by a different use of technology. STORE STORE™ presented a new industry structure organized around *demand side processes* (whose objective was to maximize the potential of each store's market area and build customer loyalty) and *supply side processes* (whose objective was to minimize the cost of replenishing product to the store or the shopper).

Offshoots of the demand-side/supply-side research included Strategic Marketing Assortments (as a way to optimize the local market performance of each store through differentiation), *Market Level Logistics* (as a way to take significant cost out of the industry pipeline), and *Management Performance Cost* (an activity-based costing model that rationalized the economics of both the supply and demand sides) — all concepts that would return the power of productive marketing and efficient product flow to the industry. SMART STORE™ has even been credited with the insights that started ECR.

All these ideas were applauded by industry leaders and applied to businesses around the world to varying extents. But the US industry's performance overall continued to decline. In fact, using 1991 as a base year (the year before ECR) through 1997, inflation-adjusted sales per square foot have dropped 17.2 percent according to *FMI Speaks* (1997).

In the United States today, forward buying and diverting are rampant, and the amount spent on trade deals is accelerating. Industry responses to the growing pressures of saturation — ECR, globalization (in Europe), and consolidation (in the US) — are only making matters worse by perpetuating the *old* industry model, a model that's increasingly inefficient and even irrelevant. As a result, price pressures continue to increase. But the simple truth is this: margins will never improve until the fundamental economics of the industry more closely match the current market realities in most developed countries; i.e., saturated markets without population growth.

It's obvious, really: the mass market economic model (which depends on constant, outward growth — *more* markets, *more* items, *more* consumers) that made this industry successful in the past just won't work in the future, particularly when the average consumer of the late 1990s wants to be treated as an *individual*. In fact, the mass market model is creating inequities, infighting, and productivity barriers that will never be fixed until we align the money that retailers and manufacturers earn with the *value* they deliver, as it's perceived by the individual shopper. Now, the industry needs to move to an alignment of value, cost, risk, and reward — an alignment that I believe started to disappear from this industry at least 20 years ago. It's this alignment that will create what I'm calling the *Frictionless Marketplace*.

I've written this book to describe the *Frictionless Marketplace* and the industry model that will make it work — the **AGENTRY Model**.

In the *Frictionless Marketplace*, retailers and manufacturers are rewarded for *working together* in delivering *true value* to shoppers. While many trends point toward the emergence of this new phase for the industry (as well as the **AGENTRY Model**), *one* will force the realignment of the industry around *shopper value*: the Internet. In fact, the Internet will free the death hold the land-based store has on this industry and will, in fact, improve this industry's marketing and logistics productivity by quantum leaps. The economics cannot be denied. The money saved by eliminating expensive and unproductive mass marketing practices will fund the shift to the new industry model.

I believe the Internet is becoming a seamless part of our everyday lives. If you don't agree, don't bother to read this book, because this belief is central to an understanding of, and acceptance of, the *Frictionless Marketplace* and the **AGENTRY AGENDA**™. The emergence of a marketing-driven industry model, supported by the Internet, will create a marketplace without friction, one in which goods, information, and money can flow freely — without impediment, without "surcharges" and barriers — among manufacturers (and other suppliers), retailers, and customers.

The next decade could be the most exciting one in this industry's history. Stores will still exist, but they'll be enjoyable places to shop and fun places to work. They'll create *moments of value* (whether solutions, information, social interactions, or entertainment) for shoppers. Manufacturers will have barrier-free access to their targeted consumers, with willing help from the retailer turned **AGENT**. Industry players will enter new markets in developing countries the right way — not by replicating today's model, but by using the **AGENTRY Model** to prevent future waste, redundancy, and saturation. And those thinking out of the "four-wall box" will make a lot of money. What a nice change!

I hope that after you've read this book, you'll find the arguments in favor of the **AGENTRY AGENDA**™ as obvious and compelling as I do. Yes, there will be "push back" from some companies, especially those manufacturers and retailers who have counted on muscle to win market share over the past few decades. True, right now, size is a competitive advantage; but in the *Frictionless Marketplace* it won't necessarily be. In fact, it could be a competitive *dis*advantage as a "perfect" logistics system levels the cost of getting products to market. On the other hand, those manufacturers who make winning products, and those retailers who earn outstanding shopper loyalty, will readily endorse the **AGENTRY AGENDA**™ because they already understand the power of marketing performance.

As you read this book, keep in mind the two most often voiced opinions at SMART STORE™: *"What a great idea. Who else is doing it?"* and *"We can't do that. We're too big."* These are not the thoughts of the companies which will survive in the *Frictionless Marketplace*.

Note: Since I don't want to be accused of gross generalization (a "mass marketing" fault I attribute to the industry with its commonly held, implicit belief in the "goodness of sameness": i.e., *every shopper is the same)*, I would like to say there are a few good exceptions to every criticism I level in this book. Many retailers today are already acting as agents *to the best of their abilities*, given the constraints of the mass marketing model. Unfortunately, only a few are public companies.

I want to thank the thousands of retail and manufacturing executives who have visited SMART STORE™ (in Chicago, Windsor, or Tokyo) over the past ten years, because the discussions I've had with them have been my inspiration in writing this book.

While my years with Andersen Consulting cannot help but have had an impact on my work and while much of the research I have drawn upon was conducted by Andersen Consulting, I wish to stress that the opinions and view expressed in this book are my own and not necessarily those of Andersen Consulting.

1   SMART STORE™ is a trademark of Andersen Consulting.

Contents

"When all men think alike, no man thinks very much."

WALTER LIPPMANN

How did we get where we are today? 1 ▪ PERSPECTIVE

INDUSTRY EXECUTIVE ASKS RELEVANT QUESTION

It's my experience that, oddly enough, a lot of executives in the industry have very little understanding of *how* or *why* the businesses they serve came to be the shape and size they are today. They know that markets are saturated with same-as stores; that stores are full of same-as products; and that shoppers often can't differentiate their stores or products from those of competitors. But frequently they don't know what the industry was like for the last generation or the one before.

It's obvious to
me that the
industry. . .has
gone through
four distinct
phases. . .

To make a case for change, we need to look back — to where we came from — because, in many ways, the **AGENTRY Model** is the best of all possible worlds, including some elements that would be familiar to our grandparents and some that will seem commonplace to our grandchildren.

It's obvious to me that the industry (first in the U.S., then in Europe, and soon in Asia) has gone through four distinct phases, each characterized by unique economics, business practices, technologies, and value propositions. Each stage has been shorter than the one before, a testimony to the speed of change that characterizes so much of modern life. I'm also convinced that we are on the brink of a completely new phase — the *Frictionless Marketplace* — whose definition is the heart of this book.

THE *Personal Touch* DURING THE 4 PHASES...

Before 1945—Pre-Development

In these simpler times, the general population is less mobile. Everyone lives in neighborhoods and shops at small, corner stores: dry goods, the butcher shop, a bakery. Service is very personal and customer-focused, but the logistics of moving product is inefficient. Getting product to the store shelf is costly, and consumer choice is very limited.

Yet, the shopping experience itself is logical. The shopper enters the store with a "problem" — *What's for dinner, tonight?* — and expects to leave with a solution. The shopkeeper — the neighborhood grocer/butcher/baker — is, really, an **AGENT**. He helps the shopper resolve her "problem" by suggesting alternative meats and complementary foods, by gathering the agreed-on items (the shopper is not responsible for the "labor" of shopping), and perhaps even by having her purchases delivered to the house. (In SMART STORE™[1] Europe, a picture of an original Sainsbury store shows stools for customers to sit on while being served.)

. . .a picture of an original Sainsbury store shows stools for customers to sit on while being served.

The grocer's "data warehouse" is between his ears!

Because branded, pre-packaged products are rare, the grocer also gathers together the right bulk items — the ones his customers want — or places special orders for those he doesn't stock. As an **AGENT**, the grocer is a go-between, a deal maker; the one who connects the buyer with the seller. The grocer's "data warehouse" is between his ears! Shopper feedback is important.

Relationships between the grocer and his customers are one-to-one; he inquires after their families, their health, their hobbies. He knows their likes and dislikes; he might help them plan menus, suggesting alternative or complementary products to complete a meal. If he says *the ham is good*, the ham is good. The shopper *trusts* the grocer and his employees. All these qualities — personal service, close attention to the individual, a high level of trust — make it highly unlikely a shopper would switch to another grocer.

I was born at the end of the Pre-Development phase, but got a good taste of what the small-store service of that time period was like when living in the Netherlands from 1975-77. In our neighborhood was a local butcher, Mr. Jaap Van Veen — *the best meat man in town*, according to my Dutch friends.

Jaap was an early practitioner of what's called *solution selling* today. His store carried regular-cut meats, partially and fully prepared meats, two or three red wines, a few types of bread; in short, carefully selected items, merchandised together to meet a defined need. (Other stores in the neighborhood did the same with fish, or cheese, or poultry, etc. — these were very efficient assortments!) He even provided barbecue grills for rent — complete with charcoal — in the summer.

Jaap would always suggest items: "*Try this wine with those lamb chops.*" Then, when the shopper returned to the store, he'd always ask, "*How did you like that wine?*" The Dutch have a name for Jaap's type of store: "*easy shopping.*"

The familiarity and service levels in Jaap's store created a huge switching barrier. In fact, his customers were so "tied" to his stores (as were their friends — everyone in the neighborhood, actually) they could leave messages for each other — "*Ask Judy to call me.*" — confident that my wife would be in the store that day or the next and that Jaap would notice and remember.

Loyal neighborhood shoppers even invited Jaap to their homes; a friend of mine, for example, asked Jaap to his 50th birthday party! Can you imagine asking the store manager of your local supermarket over for dinner? Do you even know his name?

The idea of a grocery store manager having a personal relationship with shoppers is foreign to most of today's retailers, but was certainly a way of life for the "mom and pop" who ran the neighborhood stores of the Pre-Development phase. Yet, what would better ensure loyalty than friendship, as well as a commitment to the welfare of one's neighbors?

Hard to imagine that these neighborhood stores would become the supermarkets of the 1990s. Yet, in just about every chain's headquarters (and in many stores) is a picture of this "first store," prominently on display, creating (unintentionally, I'm sure) a nostalgia for a time when the store was charming and intimate.

The economics of the Pre-Development phase. . .

- The shopping experience is logical, focused on resolving shopper's "problems" (i.e., *What's for dinner tonight?*); customer service is great; relationships are important.

- Management is decentralized; the "data warehouse" of information about customers is in the employees' heads. Employees are very important because of their knowledge of customers and judgment about products.

- The shopper is queen, the retailer her trusted **AGENT**, getting whatever is needed in daily trips to the open market.

- Food is an important (large) part of the family budget. Since the shopper goes to the store every day, the gap between the *moment of desire* and the *moment of value* (see page 102 for a discussion of this key concept) is very small.

- Product sales reps go store to store, then deliver orders to each store one case at a time. The downside is that product movement (logistics) is very unproductive and inefficient; the upside is vendors understand the marketing needs of each local store. In addition, the merchant (grocer) goes to the market early in the morning to select with care that day's fresh items for the store.

- Shopping is a social event; the store is a source of information.

1945-1975—Development (post war)

After World War II, changes in U.S. demographics and lifestyle have a dramatic impact on food retailing. Hand in hand with the Baby Boom is the mushrooming of suburban commu-

nities. People leave the cities with their corner grocery stores for areas where land is plentiful and where big, big stores reflect the optimism of the young population. Everybody has a car; the idea of "neighborhood" expands beyond recognition.

At the same time, remarkable inventions — the radio and the television — find a permanent home in the kitchens and living rooms of thousands of new houses. Manufacturers begin branding their products nationally, using the tools of modern communication to create desire and fuel demand. What is the most efficient way to make these recognized and sought-after products available to a population that's spread out and mobile?

The *supermarket* is the perfect distribution center, giving consumers exactly what they want: access to the new, branded products advertised on TV the night before. Shoppers don't

The supermarket is the perfect distribution center. . .

need a grocer to trust any more; they trust the brands. (Interestingly, private label products have a much stronger market presence in Europe today because of limitations put on advertising by media owned by the state until the mid-1970s.)

The new model is simple: central buying and distribution of standard products to a standard store, based on the assumption that every market is "standard." Precision isn't important; rather, *sameness* becomes a virtue. Remember the signature peaked roof of every A&P store? *Sameness* also encourages a hierarchical, functional organization structure built around product distribution. Growth in sales and profits is made easy by leveraging the economies of scale of central buying and logistics, as same-as stores are stamped out in virgin territory.

> **Sameness also encourages a hierarchical, functional organization structure built around product distribution.**

What about the shopping experience? Shoppers are willing to give up service for the new values of price and choice. In fact, early in this phase, a relatively high percentage of the family budget is spent on food, and homemakers have time to go to the store. Therefore, the shopper is willing to assume a lot of the burden of getting food into the house. Her labor becomes part of the mass marketing economic model. One enterprising retailer, Albert Heijn, practically gives his shoppers small refrigerators (using one of the first loyalty programs) so they can convert to a once-a-week shopping experience, thereby enabling the new model to take hold.

In this Golden Age of the supermarket, the profile of the grocer and his employees changes radically. The new *store manager* worries about efficiencies: stocking shelves, displaying new products, speeding up check out, controlling traffic in the parking lot. Standardization in brands and stores makes brawn count more than brains, and relationships with customers count for nothing at all. The face of the grocer is turned toward the manufacturer. As late as the 1960s, I remember retailers competing to be first with new products from Procter & Gamble or General Mills.

The manufacturer creates the market demand; the retailer becomes the *no-risk* distributor, embracing slogans like *"Everyday low prices on brands you can trust."* The shopping experience becomes illogical, organized by product category or "picking slots" rather than by meals. In new stores at this time, the first thing a shopper often sees — just inside the front door — is salad dressing, because it's a high-margin item. The merchandising theory? *"If the shopper has limited money, let's make sure she spends it on high-margin items."* Merchandise not as important in the retailer's mind, such as meat and produce, are often outsourced, since the retailer would rather "distribute" branded products.

With logistics being more important than either merchandising or customer service, retailers put their offices in the warehouse. Organization and business practices are driven by and focused on product distribution. No wonder that even today, we hear reference to the Food Distribution Industry!

It's the era of the "land" advantage. Stores don't change much from 1945 to 1975; they just keep getting bigger to handle

> Standardization in brands and stores makes brawn count more than brains. . .

more and more product. Layouts stay the same; so do operating objectives and performance measurements. But gradually, the customer becomes a cipher, part of a *mass market*, without much "identity" to hold on to. During the next phase — Saturation — this becomes increasingly significant (and painful) for everyone, as the focus on like-item categories pushes the shopper farther and farther out of focus.

In the 1950s, the opening of a new supermarket was a big event. I remember my mother driving a half-hour (a long trip in those days) to see the new Rini's Store in Cleveland. Even in the late 1960s when I was already working with Andersen Consulting, a high school band played at the opening of one client's new store, all 18,000 square feet!

The economics of the Development phase. . .

- Population grows at a rate of more than one percent annually from 1945 to 1975.

- Early in this period, food constitutes 23% of the average consumer's monthly expenditure. Value — i.e., predictable quality for each dollar spent — is as important as ever.

- Relatively few women work outside the home; only about 30% in 1945 and 42% in 1975.

- Regional brands become national brands, which become increasingly desirable, thanks to the reach and impact of television. Manufacturers succeed with a "push" marketing model; i.e., making these products accessible is sufficient to ensure their sale.

- The small, little stores of the Pre-Development phase can put up no resistance (despite their outstanding personal relationships) to the new supermarkets moving into virtually "empty" markets. The new *mass market* model enables rapid lateral growth from one market to another. (At the end of this period, Wal-Mart follows the same model as supermarkets, *and then some*, pushing out the small stores in small towns all over the United States).

- Shopping changes from a daily to a once-a-week job, thanks again to the packaging of national brands, the use of refrigeration, and the predictable weekly meal schedule.

- Value (in the consumer's mind) comes to be defined as the aggregation of low-cost national brands in one location. Standardized packaging makes possible self-service, a cheap alternative to the personalized service of the small store. Central distribution keeps supply chain costs low, for a while.

- Central buying and distribution, which make it efficient for retailers to replicate stores, are also cost-effective for manufacturers, too, who are spared the expense and effort of calling on and/or placing products in one-of-a-kind, independent stores.

- The *customer* (as in, *the customer is always right*) becomes a *consumer*. A whole new industry — consumer research — emerges (initiated primarily by manufacturers), as decision makers in large complex organizations (manufacturers and retailers) move farther and farther away from any *real* contact with shoppers.

- Store employees are less skilled since the "old" values — knowing the product, being familiar with the customer, providing solutions — have gone away.

1975-1990—Saturation

Not surprisingly, the supermarket system gets crowded. Huge stores rise up across the street from each other, each carrying 30,000 items — or more! — instead of the 8,000 carried when the supermarkets started. Every store looks the same. More and more, products seem the same, too. At the same time, population growth flattens. Real growth for supermarkets comes from taking business away from each other. Marketing expenditures intensify and change from obtaining new shoppers for products and stores to getting shoppers to switch from competing brands and retailers.

Real growth for supermarkets comes from taking business away from each other.

Decision making in the store becomes a source of stress for three reasons:

1. The shopper has *too much* choice, with virtually no way to differentiate one choice from another. (How do brands of detergent really differ? Worse yet, how do product line extensions differ?)

2. Making an *informed* decision means reading thousands of product labels (usually without conviction that the "knowledge" gained is worth the effort expended). What do words like *improved, enhanced, fortified*, and *extra strength* mean anyway?

3. The stores are too large, making simple navigation an exhausting effort. In this period of the industry's evolution, more and more of the burden of shopping falls to the customer: the search for items, up and down the aisles; the physical struggle with the cart, with the products, at checkout, with the bags; the quest for information; and the effort to "cut through the noise" of big stores with their excessive product choice. Despite the size of the stores, they still carry only a portion of the available products, and the land-based retailer becomes a "toll gate" in getting manufacturers' products to consumers.

...and the land-based retailer becomes a "toll gate" in getting manufacturers' products to consumers.

SHOPPER'S VIEW OF SHOPPING

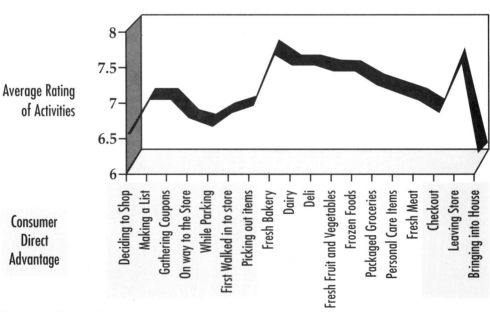

Source: Leo Shapiro and Associates

Competition among stores gets heated, as the *value* each one brings to the shopper becomes less easy to distinguish. How can a store differentiate its offerings when those offerings — nationally branded products — are available in any and every other supermarket? The ubiquitous availability of national branded products minimizes the value of the store in the consumer's mind: *"If I can get Coca-Cola anywhere, what's so special about the supermarket in my neighborhood?"* The very products that brought the supermarket into existence in the first place fail to provide them any long-term differentiation. At the same time, shoppers begin spending more and more time in the periphery of the store where fresh foods make choice meaningful (the same departments often deemed unimportant by retailers early on).

As price becomes the way many stores differentiate their value, shoppers become even more harried and confused. The question *"If I can get Coca-Cola anywhere, what's so special about the supermarket in my neighborhood?"* becomes more irksome when the customer is forced to ask, *"Where is Coca-Cola cheapest — today?"* The burden for the shopper increases, as the search for "core items" extends beyond the four walls of the store into a network of stores that must be navigated to increase the "success" of the shopping trip. A marketplace built on distributing branded products and then competing on price encourages more of the same: *more* products, *lower* prices. (The emergence of the *Frictionless Marketplace* brings this problem of price-based competition to a head once and for all — see page 42.)

By making their stores identical (and not just within chains; stores from one chain to the next are also alike for all practical purposes), retailers spread *sameness* in the industry — the *sameness* that breeds non-differentiation, boredom, and shopper disaffection. (Every store presents produce first. But is produce the center-of-plate item for most shoppers? This copycat

The very products that brought the supermarket into existence in the first place fail to provide them any long-term differentiation.

mentality inhibits retailers today, most of whom ask, *Who else is doing it?*, before trying anything new.)

Competition among manufacturers heats up, too. Limited shelf space, despite ever larger stores, gives rise to complex and costly deal structures,[2] as well as the proliferation of product line extensions; manufacturers try to elbow their products to the desirable "slots" so they might break through the "noise" and capture the eye of the wary shopper. The focus on "like item" categories in the store intensifies, while marketing tries to get shoppers to switch from one product to another when the two are often (for all practical purposes) impossible to tell apart. This "switching" focus becomes even more important as real growth in the marketplace slows.

Food retailing becomes a glutted, saturated, "same-as" industry. Saturation is everywhere: products, stores, advertising messages, logistics systems, and even ideas on how to fix the model. The economic justification of the current industry model — product acquisition and distribution — loses its value and effectiveness. Worse yet, the "consumer" (already a ghost of the former "customer") becomes almost invisible, as retailers focus even more on manufacturers' incentives as a way to make money. During saturation, the shopper is all but forgotten. For retailers, deal money is more profitable than customer service; it's assumed consumers will keep coming to the store (where else could they go?).[3]

Technology reinforces the distribution mentality as well as a centralized organization structure; the IT advantage goes to the big chains because they can afford to buy and operate mainframes. New applications — used for warehousing management and point-of-sale scanning, for example — increase the productivity of the logistics-based model. POS technology even becomes a source of income to retailers, as they sell data

For retailers, deal money is more profitable than customer service...

Technology reinforces the distribution mentality as well as a centralized organization structure...

to consumer research companies such as AC Nielsen and IRI, who in turn sell the information to manufacturers. In fact, in the very early days of the new technology, IRI gives retailers POS systems in exchange for the information generated by them. This emergence of a whole new industry — "consumer research" — results from the distance that grows between companies (manufacturers and retailers) and the people buying their products or shopping in their stores.

Saturation ... too many stores, too many products, too many logistics systems, too many deals ... no more shoppers.

SHOPPER'S CHAOS

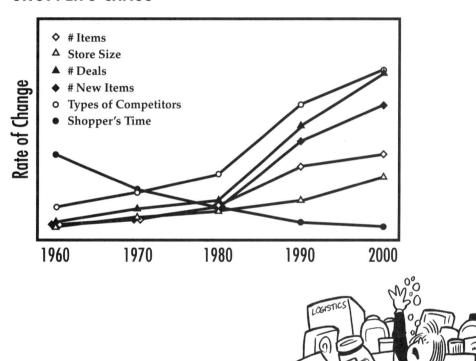

In the next ten years, all the efforts of ECR cannot undo that disastrous "cutting off" in the relationship between retailer and customer. The real — and really new — challenge becomes growth in a flat market, among shoppers who have no reason to be loyal.

The economics of the Saturation phase. . .

	1965	1995
Size of store	20,000 sq. ft	60,000 sq. ft
Number of items in store	8,000	40,000
New product introductions	Manageable	>20,000
Customer time to shop/cook	2.5 hours	< 30 minutes
Population growth rate	1.25%	.94%
Number of deals	few	thousands
Trade dollars/costs	low	$33 billion

The economic conundrum of saturation: How can a retailer or manufacturer grow (sales and revenues) when population growth is flat? And when the perceived value of national brands has been minimized by universal access to them?

The two most frequently expressed opinions at SMART STORE™ over the last ten years:

> *"What a great idea. Who else is doing it?"*

and

> *"We can't do that. We're too big."*

are representative of which of the industry's phases?

Pre-Development	☐
Development	☐
Saturation	☐
Decline	☐

(More than one answer is appropriate.)

1990-1999—Decline

Recent trends continue to undermine the distribution model of food retailing, which rests on the growth that comes from increased consumption of more and more of the same products. And, while the industry keeps looking inward, "outsiders" grab the advantage.

Population growth is flat. More than 52 percent of women ages 16-54 work full-time outside the home; an additional 17.5 percent work part-time. The traditional role of the homemaker, ready and willing to spend time and effort planning and preparing meals, is rapidly disappearing. As a friend of mine recently said, *"When my wife says, 'It's time for dinner,' the kids get up, put on their coats, and head for the car."*

> . . .while the industry keeps looking inward, "outsiders" grab the advantage.

PAVLOV'S CHILDREN

Given the constraints on the shopper's time and energy, "fast food" and alternative restaurants grab an ever-increasing percentage of "stomach share." As long as four years ago, this trend was documented in *Fortune* magazine ("The Battle for Stomach Share," May 15, 1995): Americans spend an estimated 44 percent of their income on food away from home, and nearly 50 percent of all food consumed in the U.S. is prepared outside the home. (The journalist had spent a day at SMART STORE™ and, I believe, wrote the article that kicked off the home meal replacement trend). At the end of the decade, those numbers are even higher.

At the same time, discount department stores such as Wal-Mart steal highly consumable "core items" (and shopper traffic) from the grocery stores, selling at a lower cost the branded products that were originally the very reason behind the supermarket's existence. Alternative formats use these "core items" to change the shopping habits of consumers. Products once purchased without thought from the supermarket — the

Alternative formats use these "core items" to change the shopping habits of consumers.

nationally branded products — now require some effort. Forced to shop in multiple formats and stores to get what they want, consumers are confused. *Who has the lowest price?* More than ever, that question becomes the sole point of differentiation among food retailers, and conventional grocery supermarkets can't compete with price-cutting formats. (I explain *why* later on.)

Why does it matter that food retailers lose core items to discount department stores? The answer is at the heart of decline, because the core items — available anywhere and, therefore, non-differentiating for the retailer — form the foundation for something larger and more valuable: shopper loyalty.

Retailers accuse manufacturers of unfair practices and uneven playing fields in their commerce with the Wal-Marts and clubs of the world. (Forget the fact that supermarkets had attempted the same strategy — albeit less successfully — when they tried to "steal" health and beauty products and then pharmaceuticals from drug stores in the late 1960s.) Yet, since the industry is built on the distribution of nationally branded products (with the value of its economics based on price), it's fairly understandable that manufacturers would try to help any retailer improve the supply chain. Why wouldn't they be delighted to make their products more available? Saturation is good for manufacturers! After all, saturation lowers prices; lower prices increase consumer consumption; increased consumption improves manufacturers' profits.

The same rationale — improving logistics — is used to launch Efficient Consumer Response (ECR) in 1992, which by the end of the decade has failed to deliver on its promise of significant supply chain economies. While some manufacturers improve profits (marginally) through SKU rationalization and logistics efficiencies, retailers watch their sales per square foot dive — a remarkable 17.2 percent through 1997, according to *FMI's Food Marketing Industry Speaks, 1998.* It doesn't take

. . .because the core items. . . form the foundation for something larger and more valuable: shopper loyalty.

Saturation is good for manufacturers!

a rocket scientist to figure out what that does to return on equity or return on loyal shoppers. ECR (as it's applied in the United States[4]) is about reducing costs and redistributing profits *in the old model*; it's not about aligning revenues and profits to value created for shoppers.

THE ROCKET SCIENTISTS

ECR. . .is about reducing costs and redistributing profits in the old model. . .

Retailers start to react to saturation and the need for differentiation. New merchandising strategies, such as home meal replacement and solution selling, enter into the space/value equation. But they're implemented on top of centralized, logistics-driven business practices and organizations, despite the fact that these merchandising techniques succeed only if they're sensitive to local markets. Manufacturers want to brand solutions, but not necessarily in the best interest of retailers, who need to differentiate their stores. Some retailers even bring branded "solutions," like McDonald's and Starbucks, into their stores — a strategy that attempts to stem decline, but really just prolongs the retailer's bias for distributing national brands. Within two short years, the theme at FMI's Supermarket Industry Convention & Educational Exposition shifts overwhelmingly from ECR to solution selling.

Another strategy for growth — geographic expansion, whether through consolidation or globalization — enables better "buying" within a more "efficient", centralized structure, but also spreads and increases the *sameness* in a chain and in the industry.

> ...geographic expansion,... through consolidation or globalization — enables better "buying" within a more "efficient", centralized structure...

CONSOLIDATION

Number of Grocery Retailers with 11 or More Stores

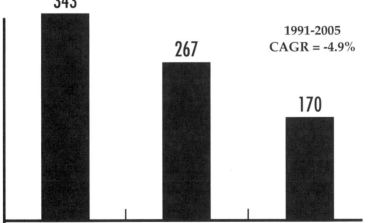

Consolidation rate based on CAGR from 1991 to 1996
Source: Chain Store Guide, Andersen Consulting analysis

Technology begins to play an ever greater role in how companies go about the "business of business."[5] As predicted in SMART STORE™ in 1990, the personal computer hits the scene and begins to change how people everywhere think about information.

Store level DSD systems are used to manage payables and the meaningless "going-in gross margin" numbers. Labor scheduling systems improve time and attendance, with a focus on productivity. Space management systems focus on like-item category efficiency, the ultimate sophistication of the shopper's "picking slot," usually done at the chain level and pushed by manufacturers. The mass marketing mindset continues. This early-on technology aims at improving *logistics* productivity; none is aimed at *marketing* objectives: increasing the local market performance of the individual store, or increasing the loyalty and profitability of each customer, or improving the shopping experience. Even POS — already in the market at this time for 15 years — just begins to extend its use beyond applications for productivity and price controls.

As distributed processing replaces mainframe number crunching, the power of information is put into the hands of local decision makers. For the first time, the IT advantage goes to small, nimble independents who can easily roll out new technology (and other changes) rather than to those large chains encumbered by centralized, slow, and expensive IT systems and complex organizations. Meanwhile, the independents apply new technology to what they know (and do) best: understanding the local market and maintaining shopper loyalty. As always, the independents lead the innovation in the industry.

Also at this time, electronic commerce begins its own "Pre-Development phase" in many industries. At SMART STORE™, the hard questions get asked: *What's the value of the land-based store in a saturated market? Could the most important "values" today's supermarket offers its customers — location and access — become irrelevant? If manufacturers can bypass the store in getting products to customers, what would happen to the trade dollars they're spending today? How will retailers make money?*

As always, the independents lead the innovation in the industry.

THE SHOPPER'S POSITION...

ON SHOPPING CART `OR` COMPUTER KEYBOARD

If nationally branded products (non-differentiating commodities) are picked, packed, and delivered out of a low-rent warehouse (the scenario of a virtual food-shopping model), the economics are excellent. In fact, analysts with the Consumer Direct Cooperative (CDC)[6] predict virtual shopping could cut $30 billion in costs out of the food retailing supply chain. (Given that today's industry annually spends $33 billion in trade promotions, this cost reduction figure might be very conservative.)

Today, shoppers are already willing to pay a little extra for convenience; the success of marketing entrepreneurs like Peapod, Streamline, and NetGrocer (see page 68) prove that conclusively. And, in the future, virtual could easily be cheaper (for the customer) than a trip to the store, especially when total costs (the expense of time, fuel, impulse buying, etc.) are calculated.[7] As I discuss later, the virtual channel by its nature drives prices for nationally branded products down to the lowest common denominator. This single fact—the diminishing importance of *land*, of a

. . .the virtual channel by its nature drives prices for nationally branded products down to the lowest common denominator.

brick-and-mortar store, and its stranglehold over the process of "buying and selling" *anything* (including food) — will be the final straw that breaks the back of our current industry model.

The Economics of the Decline phase. . .

- The current model's dependence on *land* (i.e., big stores, placed in "new" markets) continues to inhibit real growth. Manufacturers introduce new products and offer more incentives to break through the barriers created by the supermarket. Slotting allowances and trade promotion dollars account for a lot of the retailer's profits; scale becomes more important because, with size, comes more "buying power."

- In a model that promotes geographic expansion (more markets! more consumers!), there are only two possible strategies: consolidation or globalization. Both encourage better "buying" within a lower cost centralized structure; neither "solution" is in the best interests of the individual shopper (or the manufacturer), because both increase the *sameness* in a chain and in the industry, while moving decision makers even farther away from the shopper in the store.

- The new products crowd the stores even more, and each store's capacity limits the number of products (new or old) it can carry. In effect, the retailer charges the manufacturer a "toll" to enter the marketplace; products cannot compete on a level playing field; that is, on the basis of their quality or desirability alone. Innovators with good products have a hard time breaking into the business. Stores get bigger to accommodate both nationally branded items and "solutions" such as home meal replacement. But the larger stores are not reengineered to accommodate shoppers.

- The "item's shelf value" declines in the shopper's perception. Core items are everywhere, and they are the same no matter where they are sold. In fact, the manufacturer's goal is to have product *everywhere*; but this also minimizes the distribution value of the store in the shopper's mind.

- When the land goes away, what happens to the profitable tolls? Today, every retailer has to ask: *"Do I add value above and beyond distribution? How should — or could — I make my business more profitable by creating the value that would increase customer loyalty?"*

What's In a Name?

Before 1945, store keepers used the term *customer* to indicate the shopper's loyalty to their stores. (The word derives from *custom* which, according to *The American Heritage Dictionary*, can mean "habitual patronage, as of a store." I think the key word here is *habitual*. The common expression is "customer loyalty," not "consumer loyalty.") A slogan such as *The customer is always right!* shows the importance of that name; the customer relationship was a personal one in a system and an era focused on one-to-one service.

The term *consumer* emerged along with mass marketing in the Development phase. The actions and attitudes of the individual were no longer paramount; what mattered was the action and attitude of large segments of the population, segregated by data and demographics and studies through *consumer research*. This research, in turn, replaced the hands-on knowledge of the old "mom and pop" grocer, encouraging decision-makers to become increasingly distanced from contact with *real* customers.

When the alternative formats entered the fray, they tried to distinguish their place in a saturated industry by calling their shoppers *guests* and by putting *greeters* at the front door. In their advertising campaigns, these retailers always stress their friendly, helpful, *one of the family* employees. Was Jane Q. Shopper impressed? Probably not. In the public's mind there was no confusion: these stores had better prices (at least on core food items), not better service.

Maybe it's time to use the word *customer* again so we can get in touch with the roots of this industry: people "habitually" serving people, just like the Pre-Development phase.

THE LOOK OF THE CUSTOMER....

BEFORE 1945

Who is responsible for the shopping experience? When I question food retailing executives, the answer — after a moment of surprised silence — is always, *Everyone*. Buyers, marketers, category managers, store managers — they all have a piece of the shopping experience, yet they are each measured against different criteria. Clearly, if *everyone* is responsible for the shopping experience, then *no one* is. The quality of the shopping experience is not part of today's performance measurement systems. Therefore, it's not part of management's expectations, nor is it likely to be on the agenda when a company's leaders plan for the future.

PHASES OF THE INDUSTRY

	Pre Development Pre 1945	Development 1945-1975	Saturation 1975-1990	Decline 1990-2000	Frictionless 2000+
Customer Orientation	Individual Shopper	Consumer Segment	Forgotten	Who?	Individual Shopper
Core Competency	Shopper satisfaction	Logistics	Buying	Committee Meetings	Shopper Anticipation
Technology	Manual	Tabulating Machines, Early Computers	Mainframe Computers, Electronic Point of Sale	Personal Computers	Internet
IT applications	Bookkeeping	Back Office	Operations	Fine Tuning, Efficiency	Individual Marketing, Shopper Integration
Technology Advantage	No One	IBM	Big Chains	Independents	Shopper
Information Source	Employees	Accounts Payable	Point of Sale	Manufacturers	Shoppers
Retailer Orientation	Merchant	Distributor	Buyer	Deal Maker	Agent
Shopping Experience	Social	Physical	Illogical	Confusing	Enjoyable
Organization	Local	Centralized	Hierarchical	Cross Functional	Relieved
Food Focus	Bulk items	National Brands	Private Label	Solutions	Answers
Headquarters Location	Store	Warehouse	Separate Office Bldg.	ECR Meetings	Store
Industry Power	Shopper	Manufacturer	Retailer	Wall Street	Shopper
Store Employees	Knowledgeable	Strong	Expensive	Scarce	Differentiating
Key Measurement	Customer Friendship	Cases per Hour	Deal Money	Share Price	Loyalty
Manufacturer's focus	Store to Store	Buyer	Customer	Category	Shopper
Key Industry Trend	Store Performance	Growth	Consolidation	Globalization	Shopper Performance
Core Items' Role	Bulk	Enabled Self-service Supermarkets	Enabled Alternatives Formats	Enabled Consumer Direct	Enabled Level Playing Field
Profitability	Customer	Item	Category	Trade Dollars	Shopper

Endnotes

1
p. 3 SMART STORE™ is a trademark of Andersen Consulting.

2
p. 16 Initially (before POS technology), many deals took the form of "count and recount" agreements in which retailers would be paid promotion dollars for products that actually went out the door (rather than came in the door). Soon enough, the deals became too numerous for this type of record keeping to be practical. Everyone agreed to consider purchases as representative of sales performance; hence, the rise of forward buying and diverting, two expensive and wasteful practices that are bringing the logistics-based industry model to its knees. Ironically, "count and recount" agreements were the right idea, resembling scan-based trading, today's effort to bring reason back to promotions.

3
p. 16 While giving a presentation to manufacturing vice presidents of marketing, I said retailers would be wise to devote more space in the store to "periphery" products since these are the ones consumers spend time and effort buying. It's these "periphery" products (i.e., fresh foods, solutions, home meal replacements, etc.) that afford a store real differentiation, especially since all stores carry the same national branded products (the "center of the store").

An older man reacted: *"Don't retailers know where they make their money?"*

"Sure," I responded, *"Retailers know the center of the store is profitable, particularly because of trade dollars. But what about the shoppers? What do they care about? What attracts them to the store in the first place? What makes them loyal? Not the center of the store, that's for sure. And retailers sure won't get more trade dollars if they can't attract shoppers."*

4
p. 22 When industry leaders in Europe implemented ECR (or at least borrowed some of its better aspects), they did so (at my recommendation) around the demand side/supply side model first developed at SMART STORE™. I think European retailers have always been more strategic than their U.S. counterparts; for example, they were far "ahead of the curve" in offering home meal replacement solutions (and still do a better job with this today). When it came to ECR, they recognized the importance of demand side objectives; i.e., *maximize the potential of each store's market area and build customer loyalty.*

In 1994, I attended a CIES logistics meeting whose guest speaker talked about ECR in the U.S. and its objective to reduce inventory time in the pipeline from 106 days to 60 days. A member of the audience raised his hand and asked, *"Does that mean we have to go from 28 days to 60?"*

5
p. 23 FMI even starts a technology trade show, MarkeTechnics, to help its members get a grip on the new tools of performance improvement. But in the food industry — as in so many others, initially — these technology point solutions are put on top of old business practices and processes.

6
p. 25 Andersen Consulting initiated the formation of the *Consumer Direct Cooperative*, an association made up of diverse organizations — manufacturers, retailers, wholesalers, consumer direct companies, investors, academicians, technology companies, research firms, transportation companies, and others — who have an interest in identifying significant changes vis-à-vis logistics and marketing within the industry as a result of virtual shopping.

7
p. 25 In fact, David Glass, CEO of Wal-Mart, was cited as saying that Consumer Direct could be the most efficient distribution channel in the industry when he anounced Wal-Mart's virtual shoppping initiatives.

The Bad News and the Good News 2 ▪ TODAY'S INDUSTRY

When the industry embraced mass marketing, it lost touch with the shopper. Today, more than 50 percent of the space in a typical U.S. chain supermarket is still given over to branded products — the very items the shopper can *now* get anywhere.

This is problematic for a few reasons: 1) manufacturers spend more and more trade dollars, yet shoppers get less and less value from these investments; 2) ECR has as its focus the improvement of an economic model that's already in decline; and 3) the emergence of a virtual food retailing channel promises to choke out the little remaining profit of selling "core items" in a land-based store.

The one thing (the mass marketing of branded "core items") that "made" the supermarket *super* will not sustain its purpose in the future. If one could imagine an *ideal* store (and food retailing concept), what would it look like? If one were free to conceive of *any* store, would it be the supermarket of the 1970s?

Retailers and manufacturers are trying hard to break away from the saturation and decline of today's industry. Their innovations — what I call "point solutions"— hint at the characteristics of the new model — a *marketing* model — that will take the place of today's old *logistics* one. Consider them a preview of coming attractions.

Wasted Dollars

In 1997, Andersen Consulting published *The Daunting Dilemma of Trade Promotion*, the findings of a study of practices common to 30 manufacturers, 25 brokers, and 33 wholesalers and retailers.[8] The well-researched conclusion: trade promotion is unproductive, disruptive, and complex, with a dubious return on investment for anyone. Specifically, hidden costs are higher, and benefits much lower, than participants imagine. No surprise!

In 1996, the industry spent 13 percent of sales — $25 billion — on trade promotions in the grocery channel, making it manufacturers' No. 2 P&L item, second only to cost of goods. Hidden costs, incurred by both manufacturers and retailers, add on another $5-8 billion, of which 70-80 percent is attributable to supply chain volatility and uncertainty. Given flat, satu-

The one thing. . . that "made" the supermarket super will not sustain its purpose in the future.

rated markets and increasing consolidation and globalization, the problems inherent in this scenario will worsen.

Because promotion spending brings dollars into a market of pennies, retailers have adopted practices, built infrastructures and systems, and designed operating models to capture the supposed profit. "Deals" are more profitable than customer service initiatives, and the power of charging manufacturers "tolls" to gain access to consumers keeps the power of profitability in the hands of retailers with space to sell.

A manufacturer offers a case discount to meet end-of-period sales objectives. Retailers respond rationally and legally by forward buying and diverting. While each "deal" makes sense considered by itself, the aggregate effect is very problematic. For the industry as a whole, trade promotions increase the cost of warehousing, transportation, and inventory management; both the manufacturer and retailer invest in operating systems to optimize these poor practices. The result, according to IRI estimates,

. . .both the manufacturer and retailer invest in operating systems to optimize these poor practices.

CON ARTISTS CALL THIS
" SEPARATING THE FOOL FROM THE MONEY"

is an incremental increase in sales — *not profits* — of $28 billion. In other words, the industry spends $33 billion to generate $28 billion in sales. Rather than increasing profit, trade promotions actually create big losses for the entire industry.

Where's the customer in trade promotions? Nowhere.

In fact, as part of the study, Andersen Consulting interviewed 300 randomly chosen shoppers in four retail chains. The findings included these:

- 60 percent of consumers said promotions have no influence on store selection.

- Fewer than 30 percent look at weekly ads before shopping.

- Consumers were unaware that 51 percent of the promoted items they had purchased were on sale; the discount had no impact on their buying behavior.

- Of those 49 percent aware of the promotion, 40 percent would have bought the item anyway; 37 percent switched from another brand; and only 23 percent purchased product "incremental" to their regular buying behavior.

RETAILERS   MANUFACTURERS   CONSUMER

MASS MARKETING

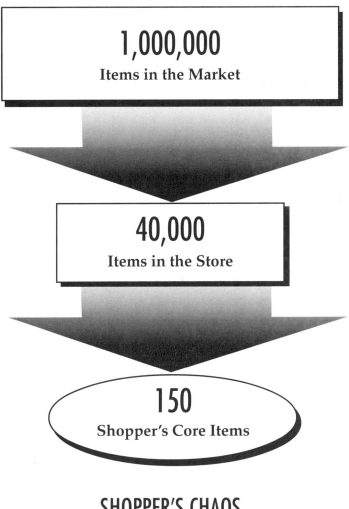

SHOPPER'S CHAOS

On top of this inefficiency, manufacturers introduce from 15,000-20,000 new products each year[9] into stores that can hold only 40,000. At the same time, the typical shopper regularly buys less than 150 "core items" (i.e., those items making up a large percentage of annual purchases), which don't change often. The industry's obsession with deals and price competition forces customers to go from store to store, looking for the best price on core items — a direct affront to any concept of loyalty. Additionally, manufacturers continue to push volume on consumers, who are increasingly unable to distinguish the value of products which are crowded into stores where choice has become a burden. When money changes hands, but no value is created, false economics are created; the industry can only suffer in the end.

When money changes hands, but no value is created, false economics are created; the industry can only suffer in the end.

When mass marketing meets brick and mortar, every store looks the same.

Has anyone ever entered a U.S. chain supermarket without turning into produce, rounding the corner to meat, finishing off around the edges in dairy, then plunging up and down the aisles to find packaged goods, organized by some logic that has nothing to do with utility?

Early in the Development phase (1945-1975), distribution of then-new branded products was so important that many retailers "outsourced" their meat and produce offerings and operations. By far the largest part of the store was given over to the nationally branded items. It still is. More than half of the typical store's space is used for packaged (branded) goods, despite growing evidence shoppers spend most of their time in the store around the peripheries (in fresh foods areas), where their decisions are meaningful. If a customer always buys Tide detergent, what's the value in him or her making that choice in the aisle of a supermarket? By definition, the better the nationally branded product, the more it's non-differentiating. Customers will not pick one store over another if they both carry the same core item, assuming price is neutral. The two retailers might have to carry it, but it alone doesn't make one retailer more attractive to the shopper. A store layout designed 40 years

. . .the better the nationally branded product, the more it's non-differentiating.

ago, when shoppers' values were very different, still has a grip on the industry today. We are biased by our past.

> **W**hy is it so hard to buy plastic bags? Has anyone ever bought the *right* bag on a first try? Too many choices, not enough differentiation. Yet, MBAs spend a lot of energy on this section of the store (and others like it), optimizing its space and profit performance without thinking about helping the consumer pick the *right* bag. Why not have samples on display?

What Went Wrong?

Why didn't the $30 billion savings promised by Efficient Consumer Response (ECR) materialize? Granted, some manufacturers' (primarily core item manufacturers) profits have improved through SKU rationalization and logistics efficiencies, and many retailers have improved their bottom lines a bit. But remember, when we look at supermarket sales per square foot, using 1991 as a base year and adjusting for inflation through 1997, we see a glaring 17.2 percent *decline* (See chart page 38).

The 1992 Alternative Format Study, presented at FMI's Midwinter Conference, looked at the threat of alternative formats: discount department stores, discount drug stores, and club stores — selling nationally branded food products (the raison dêtre of the supermarket). The study concluded that the alternative formats, because their gross margins and operating costs were lower on a percentage basis, were more efficient (particularly in logistics and related business practices) than traditional grocery stores (See chart page 40).

In my opinion, that conclusion was wrong. As an old-time merchant told me early in my career, "*You don't put percentages in the bank.*" He was right in many ways, not only from a finan-

...marketing
productivity of
alternative
formats is much
more efficient.

cial basis but from a marketing basis as well. The right conclusion to the *1992 Alternative Format Study* is that the *marketing productivity* of alternative formats is much more efficient. What do I mean? The alternative formats are successful because they 1) cherry-pick the top-performing items in a supermarket category, 2) reduce prices in response to the selected items' turnover efficiencies, and 3) lower prices even more on these core items to create traffic for other, higher margin departments and to build overall store loyalty. Naturally, larger profits result.[10] (The supercenters are just a more sophisticated version of the same marketing strategy; they use the whole food portion of the store to build traffic for the total store. I understand that the marginal lift in sales of the higher margin, nonfood sections can exceed $100,000 a week, when a discount store is converted to a supercenter. That's a lot of marginal margin!)

WEEKLY SALES PER SQUARE FOOT

	1991	1992	1993	1994	1995	1996	1997
Actual	$9.80	$9.70	$9.60	$9.18	$9.27	$9.78	$9.45
Inflation Adjusted	$7.22	$7.09	$6.85	$6.37	$6.23	$6.34	$5.98
Percent Decline, 1991 Base		1.8%	5.1%	11.7%	13.7%	12.2%	17.2%

Source: Food Marketing Institute

Instead of viewing top-performing categories as "stand-alone business units," the alternative formats make them part of the store's overall marketing strategy. The logistics advantages are only a *by-product* (although substantial) of their success in marketing. I doubt that Wal-Mart's warehouse workers pick individual cases any faster than Kroger's do; rather, the marketing strategies for the store — including the role of categories — enable the alternative formats to use *efficient product handling patterns* to generate *additional* profits. For example, since they carry only selected high-volume items, they can ship products by pallet, using cross-docking (a technique that's been around for years in non-food distribution) for store delivery rather than picking cases in a warehouse. As a result, the average supermarket — which carries the complete category, including the "dogs," with no other high-margin categories in the store, or no other means to differientiate — is at risk. And what's worse, when the supermarket loses its core items, it loses the loyalty of its shoppers.

In addition, ECR's definition of "alternative formats" is wrong because it is too restrictive. What about other businesses which compete for the meal? The term "alternative formats" should include restaurants and foodservice providers like fast-food chains. In most cases, ECR has overlooked these formats, even though they've made substantial inroads in gaining a "share of stomach." Even ECR's definition of categories is too structured. Which makes more sense from the shopper's perspective: the *cereal* category or the *breakfast* category? Our "Development phase" mindset won't let us think outside the center-of-the-store box. I'm afraid that ECR focused on the non-differentiating, declining portion of the declining segment of the food industry.

I think the year 2000 will mark the end of today's mass marketing, logistics-based model. ECR has tried hard to extend the life of the model, but innovation will win as the breakaway force behind the success of future food retailers. Innovation will drive the industry to a new model. And that innovation will be everywhere: new products, new services, and new shopping experiences; in other words, new ways of creating differentiated shopper value.

> . . .ECR focused on the non-differentiating, declining portion of the declining segment of the food industry.

THE MISLEADING PERCENTAGES

	Grocery	Mass	Discount Drug	Club
Gross Profit	25.3	25.0	20.0	11.0
Operating Expenses	21.8	17.5	16.0	7.5
Profit Margin	3.5	7.5	4.0	3.5

The Forces of Change By applying Michael Porter's Five Forces Model, *Competitive Strategy*, Free Press, 1998, to the individual store, we can see what's wrong in the current industry model.

PORTER'S FIVE FORCES MODEL

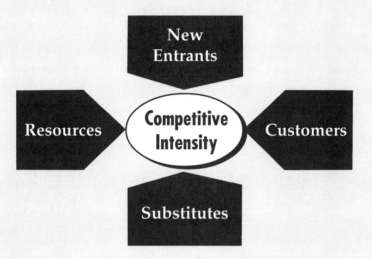

The first force is **customers** (shoppers): their choice and sophistication increase as the amount of information available to them increases. The threat here includes everything from advertising to the Internet — a force of change that's accelerating rapidly. In today's industry, the customers are in real power because there are fewer of them per store (the overall population is not growing) and because saturation gives them more options to pick from.

The second force driving the competitive intensity of a store is **new entrants**. With saturation and alternatives formats (resulting in a 17.2% decline in sales per square foot), this is obviously a threat.

The third force — **substitutes** — is also clearly present in the battle for stomach share being waged by stores, fast-food chains, "boutiques" like Starbucks, home shopping, and conventional restaurants.

The Forces of Change (continued)

Finally, the last force is the store's control over its **resources**, of which two are particularly important: products and employees. The employee "resource" has been (and will remain) a threat for a long time. As long as I can remember, it has been hard (generally speaking) for supermarkets to attract and keep motivated people (exceptions include stores like Wegmans, Ukrop's, Superquinn, and Dorothy Lane). The store's access to product, on the other hand, is under no threat. In fact, the stores are swamped with too much product and the offer of money to carry them.

But where has ECR spent its efforts? On the one force that's not a *threat* to a store's competitive intensity — cleaning up the *current* supply chain, driven by core item manufacturers. Why didn't ECR start with produce, or deli, or other differentiating areas? The area where shoppers spend their time. Is it because there were no trade dollars or trade-dollar interference then? Or because there isn't any manufacturer support? Or is it because the "fresh" supply chain needs to be *really* efficient or the product spoils?

All the other forces (and threats) are marketing-related, including, in my opinion, the recruitment and retention of employees (associates). The loss of business in the industry is caused by marketing faults; unfortunately, the distribution-centric model and trade dollars are insensitive to *external* threats directed at the shopping experience.

The Price Death Spiral

In the Development phase, the supermarket achieved dominance by selling nationally branded products 20 percent cheaper than the corner store. It could do this because of centralized buying and distribution, product and store standardization, and shopper self-service. In the early history of the supermarket, price defined value. Is it any surprise, then, that

today's retailers respond to any new idea with the question,
"How will that affect price?"

PRICE COMPETITION DEATH SPIRAL

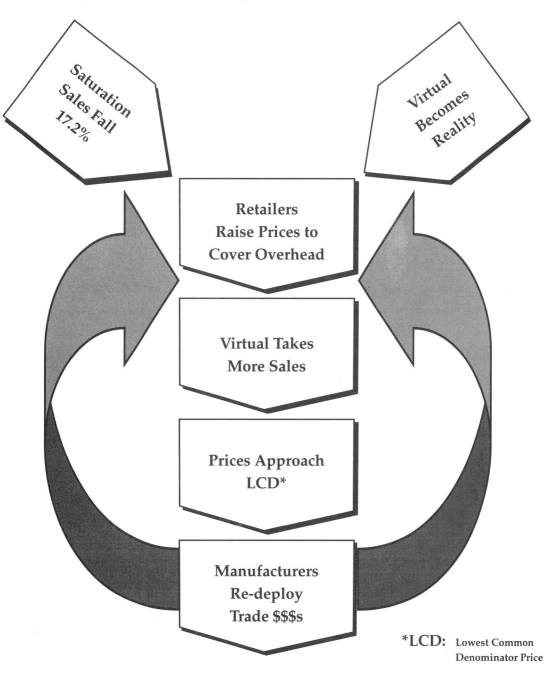

Saturation Sales Fall 17.2%

Virtual Becomes Reality

Retailers Raise Prices to Cover Overhead

Virtual Takes More Sales

Prices Approach LCD*

Manufacturers Re-deploy Trade $$$s

*LCD: Lowest Common Denominator Price

Today, prices (for nationally branded products, particularly core items, which hardly differentiate a store) are being driven down to the lowest common denominator for two reasons: 1) saturation allows national and global retailers to set prices for everyone (and set them low, a lá Wal-Mart); and 2) virtual shopping lets a "wired" consumer compare prices effortlessly, always finding the least expensive provider of a product or service. I call this "one-click comparative shopping."[11]

Can a land-based store continue to compete on nationally branded products within today's model? In any given market, operating costs (land, labor, construction, technology, etc.) for all retailers are about the same. And the purchase price of product is about the same.[12] That leaves two options: 1) **Carry a very limited selection of product (cherry-picking the high performers only)**. Rapid turnover makes up for a lower retail price. Logistics costs and organization processes are lower because replenishment (by pallet) of a few items makes everything simple. Aldi is a good example of this strategy. 2) **Use the yield approach**, allowing low prices on certain items (usually core items) to create a price image and to generate traffic, and then make up profits (and return on equity and overall space) with high-margin items. This approach is used when the retailer wants to offer a large selection of merchandise. Wal-Mart is an example of this strategy. Carrefour is a good example of using both techniques that work well in developing countries.

Increasingly built into the profit equation are trade promotion dollars/costs, representing 13 percent of manufacturers' sales — a staggering $25 billion ($33 billion in total cost) in 1996! Why? Because, in the current system, manufacturers of strong national products are rewarded for saturating markets. Saturation causes prices to fall and consumption to increase. Products become more available, in more places, more often. The retailer actually subsidizes the manufacturer's profits by

The retailer. . . subsidizes the manufacturer's profits by selling popular core item products sometimes below their total costs. . .

selling popular core item products sometimes below their total costs (including transportation, handling, storage, etc.). Retailers have to carry less popular or infrequently purchased items (which are less price-sensitive) to boost their profits through managing the yield to cover the overhead of the store's real estate investment. These products, in effect, subsidize the "core items" as well. This is hardly matching revenues with value created!

Now let's add virtual shopping to the escalating pressure of saturation. The yield equation, as it's applied to floor space, becomes irrelevant because, in the virtual world, prices will be set differently. The need to cover "space cost" is almost gone; pricing will be based on "cost to serve". Once the investment in the shopper's electronic interface is covered, pricing will focus on covering the variable distribution costs of getting the item to the shopper and of generating profits accordingly. Prices will be set virtually, not in the local neighborhood; most important, they'll be set based on product and distribution values. Amazon.com is already a good example.[13]

The impact of virtual shopping on today's stores will be huge. If the supermarket loses just 10 percent of its sales, profits turn to losses. And this 10 percent will disappear across-the-board, not just in one category or one section of the store. Of course, virtual shopping will attack the high-margin items in the land-based yield formula as well as core items. As the retailer raises prices to make up for the loss of profit, the virtual store becomes even more attractive. The trade dollars/costs, all $33 billion, will start to go away. Manufacturers (and their money) will follow the path of least resistance to shoppers, thereby forcing the land-based retailer to raise prices *again* to cover overhead. And the spiral continues. Sales will decline; profits will fall even faster. Virtual shopping will expose all the false economics in our in-

Manufacturers (and their money) will follow the path of least resistance to shoppers. . .

Virtual shopping will expose all the false economics in our industry.

dustry. Without a new way of doing business, retailers won't make any money.

Retailer, ask yourself: *What happens if I can't use yield to manage profits? What happens if I can't use limited selection to drive price? What happens if I need to compete not within each store's trading area, but nationally? What happens if the trade dollars I depend on go away or are paid only for real performance?* Manufacturer, ask yourself: *What happens if retailers don't subsidize my product any longer? What happens if my product doesn't need to subsidize other products? What will I do with all the trade dollars?*

Yet, if virtual selling is done the right way — according to the **AGENTRY AGENDA**™ — profits will flow to those who create the best shopping experience and who make the best products. Manufacturers will redirect that 13 percent spent on trade promotions and switching to reduce product costs or to create more real growth through targeted marketing and loyalty building. The **AGENT'S** actual stores will differentiate their value in ways other than price competition for nationally branded products. The customer loyalty won in the actual store will transfer to the virtual channel, and vice versa.

Numbers Don't Lie

- U.S. supermarket annual sales are about $400 billion.
- Profits are about three percent before taxes, $12 billion.
- Trade dollars spent each year equal about $25 billion, about two times more than the retailers' pre-tax profits.
- Is it any wonder retailers are dependent on manufacturers?

The economics of Mass Marketing. . .

- In today's industry, there are more than one million active items.

- In the U.S., food manufacturers introduce about 20,000 new products annually.

- The average grocery store holds 40,000 products.

- Of these, 5,000 make up at least 80% of the retailer's sales.

- The typical shopper buys less than 150 core items, again and again.

- These make up as much as 70% of his or her annual purchases.

- The industry spends an estimated 1.1% of annual sales per year on advertising and promotions, trying to create desire for those one million items.

- As a result, the shopper is bombarded with 3,000 promotion messages per day.

- The trade dollars spent to push product through "the funnel" to a flat population is the root cause of poor productivity in the industry.

- Over the past six years, grocery retailers in the U.S. added thousands of new stores to an already saturated market.

- Sales decline 17.2% per square foot (1991-1997).

Logistics Is Dead

In his book, *The Empty Raincoat,* 1994, Charles Handy of the London Business School proposes The Sigmoid Curve, an S-curve concept to describe the life cycle of a product, company, or industry. According to the S-curve concept, a product (or industry) goes through a predictable development: from its introduction to market ramp-up (with the rapid gains in productivity and profitability that come with "newness") through maturity and, eventually, decline (when sales are flat or declining). Does this sound familiar?

...the life cycle of the logistics-based, mass marketing model has run its course...

Early in the Development phase, the food industry began to climb a Logistics Productivity S-curve. In the following decades, productivity was high. So were rewards. But saturation caused logistics productivity to level off and then — gradually — begin to decline. In other words, the life cycle of the logistics-based, mass marketing model has run its course; rather than being a source of productivity gain, it has become a drag on efficiency (saturation of logistics systems) in each developed market. In fact, it has become a drag on marketing productivity as well.

WHO DESIGNED THIS? (Today's Logistics Model)

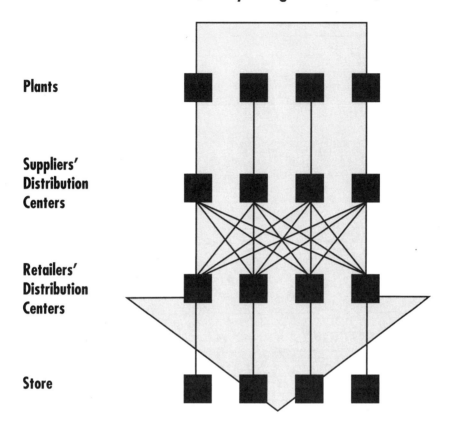

Plants

Suppliers' Distribution Centers

Retailers' Distribution Centers

Store

Handy also believes companies (or industries) typically do *not* recognize when they are at the top of a Sigmoid Curve (i.e., when they are poised for decline) because often their economic performance has never been better and because usually the momentum of past success is difficult to stop. Investments in fixed assets, business practices, and organizational culture are hard to change. Surely, this describes food retailing today. ECR was introduced to fix a problem that is, essentially, "unfixable" because mass marketing productivity has run its course. Why benchmark best practices in processes that have already peaked in their value? Why *improve* a practice that should be eliminated? Manufacturers and retailers continue

> ECR was introduced to fix a problem that is, essentially, "unfixable". . .

to spend millions on mass marketing at a time when shoppers want to be treated as individuals.[14] Despite a temporary and minor gain in logistics productivity in the mid-'90s (as a result of ECR), the industry cannot squeeze any more value out of the distribution model. In fact, I'm afraid we are already slipping *down* the logistics productivity Sigmoid Curve.[15]

LOGISTICS S-CURVE

Clearly, a *new* S-curve is needed to keep the industry moving forward (instead of continuing down the slope of the Logistics S-curve, which would be disastrous). This new S-curve is a **Marketing** Productivity S-curve on which real profits are earned by adding value for consumers (newcomers have already jumped right on it, unencumbered with the old logistics structures and mindset). Because of saturation and the Internet, location and low logistics cost *alone* will no longer be competitive advantages.

THE SIGMOID CURVE*

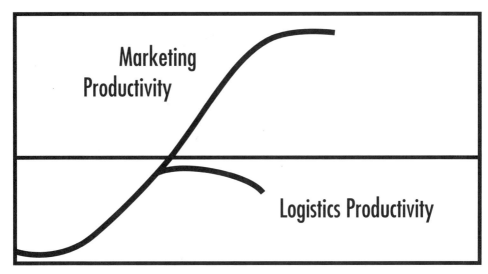

Charles Handy, The Empty Raincoat, Hutchinson/London 1994

This conclusion is already evident today. Two stores near each other (a very common situation in our over saturated markets) have the same cost structure: the same cost of land, labor, technology, inventory. While one might sell Budweiser cheaper one week, the other will do so the following week. Meanwhile, other products are priced a few cents higher or lower to create a profitable overall yield. Overall and over time, the costs clearly average out. Today, real competitive advantage comes from the quality of the shopping experience. That fact will just become more apparent in the future.

Who's already started up the Marketing Productivity S-curve? Among food retailers, companies like eatZi's, Ukrop's, Wegmans, Dorothy Lane, and Superquinn. What do they have in common? Great stores, great shopping experiences, great staff, and a sensitivity to the shopper's desire for *solutions* — for convenience and ease in shopping; access to the items they want; control of the shopping experience; home meal replacements or ready-made meals; and information about new products, meal planning, and nutrition. They are merchants, not distributors.

Once a few leaders make some headway up the Marketing Productivity S-curve, even the alternative formats (which sent everyone into such a spin) won't be threatening because they're just another form of mass marketing. And, on the *new* S-curve, the business practices and organization of mass marketing are dead. So is logistics as a competive advantage.

> As the old saying goes, *timing is everything*. Waiting too long to start up the Marketing Productivity S-curve will make catching up later impossible. Don't ask, *Who else is doing it?* As I discuss a bit later, the switching barriers in the new Marketing Productivity industry — the *Frictionless Marketplace* — will be high, very high.

U.S. GROCER'S PRIORITIES

	1998	Change from 1997
Prepared Meals	88%	-3%
Perishables	88	+1
Frequent Shopper Program	76	+6
Customer Service	75	n/c
Category Management	**72**	**-11**
Food Service	68	+2
Private Label	67	-5
Samples/Demonstrations	60	+1
Exciting Specials	51	+10
Premium Private Label	44	-2

When *Supermarket News* recently reported on the strategic priorities of food retailers, only one in ten (ranking #5) was ECR-focused or logistics-related — **category management** (also, interest in "category management" had declined 11 percent from the year before). Every other priority implies differentiation is a *marketing* challenge and opportunity. Prepared foods, perishables, frequent shopper programs, and customer service ranked higher. This is good news. Leaders are recognizing *logistics is dead* and *marketing is the new differentiating competitive advantage*. This shift in focus suggests a dawning recognition that the "shopping experience" is the only real way to win the hearts and minds of shoppers for the long term. Yet, the industry still has a long way to go to change its business practices to match this new vision.

> Leaders are recognizing logistics is dead and marketing is the new differentiating competitive advantage.

Long Live Marketing

Many independent retailers (not encumbered with logistics) — such as Dorothy Lane, Ukrop's, D&W, Superquinn, and Dick's Supermarket — are leading the industry in trying to break out of saturation through marketing innovations. Big chains are trying to do the best they can, but their efforts are necessarily limited because the underlying logistics model and (more importantly) the related, centralized organizations make true *marketing* efficiencies impossible. The "big guys" are also always confused by the aggressive category focus of the manufacturers, which detracts from the shopping experience and the potential uniqueness of each store.

That said, let's look at six "point solutions" which have the right idea (i.e., *putting the shopper first, creating a satisfying shopping experience*, and *matching revenues with value created*): **loyalty programs** (which actually reward loyal shoppers); **scan-based trading** (which eliminates forward buying and diverting); **solution selling** (which satisfies the individual shopper's need for control and answers); **activity-based costing** (which aligns value with processes/functions); **third-party logistics** (which allows stores to differentiate without incurring huge distribution costs); and **consumer direct** (which hints of the promise of a *Frictionless Marketplace*).

#1 Loyalty Programs

Independents tend to run loyalty programs the *right* way because their businesses are built on — and compete on — *relationships*. These programs reward faithful customers; they aren't used to buy new ones. In fact, these retailers had loyal shoppers before they had loyalty programs.

To make sense, a loyalty program should: 1) Attract the best shoppers for the store, those local market customers who match the "target profile" of the store and who would be loyal to a store that recognized their individuality. (Are today's loyal shoppers the targeted shoppers?); and then 2) retain these shoppers as customers by providing the best shopping experience.

Maybe the store should have first-class checkout lines for regular customers. How about a greeting from the store manager? How about loyalty pricing on "favorite" items — a private continuous sale, as it were? How about measuring promotional performance not with total sales but with top-tier shoppers' response to the sale items, including their impact vis-à-vis total purchases? While innovative independents do these types of loyalty activities (remember, they have the advantage of being able to use technology in only one or two stores), the large chains tend to look at loyalty as just a refinement of the mass marketing model. For this reason, they focus on price and trade dollars. Just about every retailer has a loyalty program, and just about every shopper has two or three loyalty cards; yet almost all the marketing dollars spent by manufacturers and retailers are still focused on making consumers "switch" rather than on keeping customers loyal. That worked 40 years ago, in unsaturated markets with a growing number of consumers who had time to shop. But long-term survival now depends on customer loyalty. Let me share an example:

Last June, at an antique show I noticed a woman selling new subscriptions to the Chicago Tribune for a special offer: $2.10 per week, instead of the standard price of more than $4.00. Being a 20-year subscriber — in my opinion, a perfect candidate for a "loyalty reward" — I asked if I could participate in the special. The answer was a resounding no. I — loyal customer — would have to cancel my subscription for 30 days to qualify. Now, that's an invitation to switch to another paper! Why be loyal when switching pays? The lesson learned: Even though loyal customers cost a company less to serve than do

Just about every retailer has a loyalty program, and just about every shopper has two or three loyalty cards. . .

. . .marketing
focuses on getting
other buyers to
switch rather than
on keeping
current customers
happy.

new customers, marketing dollars are rarely spent on them. In fact, marketing focuses on getting other buyers to switch rather than on keeping current customers happy. When should we reinvest in a loyal shopper? Isn't this more important when there are — for all practical purposes — no new shoppers?[16]

When SMART STORE™ conducted focus groups in Europe and the United States to find out about shopper needs, expectations and behavior, one middle-aged man in England said, "Of course, I'm a loyal shopper: I have four loyalty cards, and I use them all." Shoppers' skepticism about loyalty programs was confirmed by this focus-group research. Here are more points raised during the research:

- The shared perception about "preferred shopper programs" is that everybody has one. The cards are perceived as glorified check-cashing cards that grant some additional discounts. In addition, if nearly all shoppers have the cards, many participants suggest that merchants should just offer everyday low prices to everybody and eliminate the cards altogether.

- In both markets, shoppers have a jaded attitude, considering the cards just a gimmick. One chain was perceived as raising prices artificially so the stores can give discounts back to customers on specific items.

- Users also find the cards inconvenient; they forget to take them to the store (and lose out on the discounts); the card slows them down at checkout; the card creates a confusing receipt.

- The "preferred shopper programs" are appealing when the benefit is tangible, such as cash rebates (e.g. $5 for every $250 spent). Importantly, this seems to engender loyalty.

Another "loyalty" strategy which independent retailers use wisely is rewarding employees for building customer loyalty.[17] In one small chain I know of, half the store manager's bonus depends on nurturing customers who commit a significant percentage of their shopping expenditures to the store. These managers know their customers! And they know loyal customers mean long-term wealth creation, which independents typically value more than quick profit. (In defense of public companies, the shareholder pressure to show quarterly returns makes it hard to invest in the future. But that doesn't make it right! In fact, as you will see later on, I believe that if companies don't invest in the future, there will be no future for them.)

. . .loyal customers mean long-term wealth creation. . .

I had the pleasure of taking a few European grocery retailers to visit a U.S. supermarket. Within minutes of our entering the store, the manager came to greet us. I'm sure he thought that four guys in suits could mean only two things: headquarters or competitors. Well, I got to shake the hand of the store manager, even though I've never spent a dime in his store. My wife, on the other hand, has never met him. Yet, I bet she's spent $100,000 in his store over the past 20 years. Amazing! An independent retailer would not make this mistake.

etailers could learn a lesson or two from the airlines. Of course, all airlines have frequent flyer programs with virtually identical payoffs and restrictions. For someone who flies as much as I do, it's 'six of one, half dozen of another.' Then, why have I given all my business — five million miles of flying — over the past 20 years to American Airlines? Two words: Ginny Barowski. I called her the Chief Passenger Service Officer at O'Hare Airport. The attention she gave me as a customer was unsurpassed — and unsurpassable. She would recognize me on the concourse (she wasn't in the office) and call me by name. She got me on planes that were sold out. Her only question was, "What kind of seat do you want, aisle or window"? Same planes from one carrier to another; one different person! And Ginny was doing this before American started a frequent flyer program. No wonder American Airlines named a concourse at O'Hare after her when she retired.

Loyal Customers are Profitable Customers

The chart on page 59 (modified for the industry) and its explanation come from an excellent book, *The Loyalty Effect* by Frederick F. Reichheld (Harvard Business School Press, 1996). I recommend that you all read the book. Reichheld explains that the first step in understanding the "economics of customer retention" is to "quantify and profile the entire life cycle of profits" a business (retailer or manufacturer) earns from its customers. (In other words, a customer is not a $25 transaction.) His point is simple, but profound: getting a new customer costs more than keeping an old one. In fact, mature customers typically generate *additional* revenue for a business through referrals (pages 39-50 of Reicheld's book).

Acquisition cost: The money invested to bring new customers in the door. For a retailer, these costs might include the expense of opening a new store in a new market; the effort of

SHOPPER'S LIFECYCLE

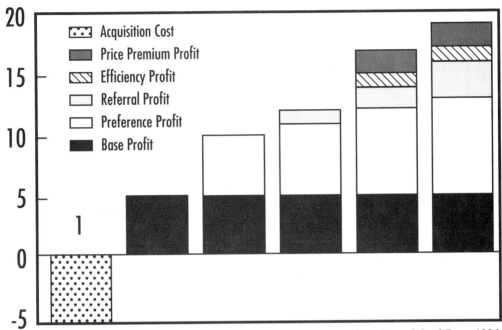

Source: The Loyalty Effect, *by Frederick F. Reinheld, Harvard Business School Press 1996*

developing a solution; loss-leader pricing to encourage switching; and — maybe the most important — employee training. But does the food retailer really know what it costs to attract each new customer? Or even what attracts the customer, price and location aside? Acquisition costs increased in the Saturation phase because of flat population growth. "Switching" marketing tactics means that acquisition costs are incurred many times. As a friend of mine used to say about smoking, "*It's easy to quit; I've done it many times.*"

Base profit: The profit unaffected by time, loyalty, efficiency, or other considerations. For a retailer, I believe this means "core items," those products that make up a large percentage of a shopper's purchases and that create a foundation of trust. And why did supermarkets let alternative formats steal their shoppers by selling core items for less?

Preference profit: As Reichheld says, one advantage of holding onto customers is (in most businesses) that their spending increases over time (especially if the service is good). In the auto service industry, for example, the average annual revenue per customer triples between the first and fifth years. Some businesses — such as credit card companies — have done a good job of accelerating the customer's movement to maturity through a combination of rewards and pricing. For supermarkets, this means merchandising to the local market and even the individual shopper. The greater a retailer's (or manufacturer's) knowledge of its customer, the greater the opportunities to sell products and services and to build on its relationships. This knowledge will become more important for the profitable selling of solutions. When the right degree of trust is established with the shopper, the retailer can even grow by offering products or services outside the traditional scope of the industry. A case in point: Retailers in the UK are offering financial services to customers. The lesson learned: core items are essential in creating loyal relationship to build on.

Referral profit: Satisfied customers recommend the business to others. Customers who show up on the strength of a personal recommendation tend to be of a higher quality, i.e., more profitable and loyal. And, clearly, acquisition costs are low. Referrals are a good way to target new customers. In fact, in a supermarket, referrals tend to be target shoppers since they are frequently friends or relatives with the same lifestyles and other similar marketing attributes of current loyal shoppers.

Efficiency profit: As customers get to know a business, they become more efficient buyers. For example, they're familiar with the services the company provides. Customer loyalty can lower operating costs as a result. For supermarkets, this could mean better scheduling of services to match the shopping habits of loyal customers. In one independent's store, for example, the premier customers tend to shop from 10:00 a.m. to 12:00 noon every day. During these hours, every checkout lane is open. The rest of the time, employees are scheduled more traditionally.

"In most industries, the cost benefits of loyalty spiral directly from the way long-term customers and long-term employees interact and learn from one another. Repeat customers tend to be pleased with the value they receive, and their satisfaction is a source of pride and energy for employees. Motivated employees stay with the company longer and get to know their customers better, which leads to still better service, builds still greater customer satisfaction, and further improves the relationship and the company's results. This human factor, personal loyalty, is powerful." (page 46 of Reichheld's book)

Does this apply to supermarkets? You bet.

Price premium profit: Old customers pay, in effect, higher prices than new ones, often because of "trial discounts" available only to brand-new customers. In food retailing, loss leaders make up a small fraction of the old customer's shopping basket. Or, as the Andersen Consulting study of trade promotions found, "specials" are really not very important to loyal shoppers: either they didn't notice an item was reduced, or they would have bought it anyway. When a customer is comfortable with a store, and when the shopping experience is positive, the real questions are, *Was the money well spent? Do I feel good when I leave the store? Do I want to come back?* In other words, values other than price are important, too.

Note: I highly recommend reading *The Loyalty Effect* for examining loyalty programs in place today in the food industry. But after reading Reichheld's logical way of looking at loyalty, one thought came to my mind. Once a customer is acquired, a business cannot assume that customer's loyalty forever. In the life cycle of a shopper, it is very important to reinvest continually in the relationship to sustain loyalty. When and how is another question.

#2 Scan-based Trading

...the retailer gets ...a "distribution" fee. . .and the manufacturer gets the rest of the revenue.

To date, a few retailers and manufacturers have collaborated on scan-based trading. In a research project sponsored by the Grocery Manufacturers of America (GMA), several manufacturers and retailers agreed to "postpone" being paid for a product until a customer buys it. When the product is actually sold, the retailer gets — in effect — a "distribution" fee (it happens to equal the gross margin), and the manufacturer gets the rest of the revenue. The retailer takes no inventory risk, and there's no reason or opportunity to "forward buy" products since promotional allowances are handled in the same manner. However, the retailer still must take the marketing risks in matching products to local-market shoppers' needs.

Perhaps even more important, scan-based trading proposes a radical economic concept — what I called in the preface a real alignment of value and reward (even though that lofty goal was not its original intention). Both the manufacturer and the retailer are rewarded only when they satisfy the shopper's *moment of value* (see page 102 for a discussion of this key concept). This eliminates many false economics associated with buying and reselling.

This eliminates many false economics associated with buying and reselling.

Key to the success of scan-based trading is information — freely shared — about local market profiles and the effectiveness of in-store promotions by product and by store. The by-products could include the ability to do activity-based costing, reduce paperwork, and improve business processes, thereby decreasing the cost of getting the product on the shelf.

Later, I'll explain why I don't like scan-based trading, as implemented today.

#3 Solution Selling

Quite a few food retailers and manufacturers are trying to provide more value to their customers through *solution selling*: the pulling together of products, information, and services in such a way that meets the particular needs of — and creates value for — targeted shoppers.[18] For example, a solution might be:

- A home meal replacement suggested for each night of the week, whether ingredients and recipes, packaged together and ready-to-fix, or the meal itself ready-to-eat (resembling *takeout* from a restaurant).

- Nutritional information, recipe demonstrations, cooking classes, or new product sampling.

- New ideas for fixing old favorites (such as "10 ways to cook chicken").

- Theme centers, such as a breakfast center, a southwestern center, a vegetarian center, a baby care center, or even a "winter cold" center (including everything from aspirin to home-made chicken soup).

- Party planning and catering (perhaps even including the rental of service pieces).

Also, "solutions" can be used to sell non-food products. How about a solution for laundry problems, or for refinishing a floor, or for picking out the right plastic bag? Why are garbage bags, and lunch bags, and leaf bags all together anyway? That's manufacturing and logistics thinking, not marketing ("shopper logical") thinking. My Dutch grocer, Jaap (see page 5), offers his customers "barbecue solutions" in which he includes not only the meat — ready for the grill — but also the grill itself (to be borrowed and returned) and the charcoal. He even cooks sometimes!

Guess what? Price is not as important as value in solution selling. In fact, how would the shopper compare price at all? In a "solution," price is variable. Twenty-four ounces of Coca-Cola or Pepsi on a shelf in a supermarket cost a lot less than they do at a lunch counter in the same store. The same amount of soda as part of a "value meal" will likely cost three or more times as much (and usually only one "cola" will be offered at the lunch counter). Also, in the store, the price is further eroded by competitive practices. It's all a question of *moment of value* (see page 102). The same product, in two different "times and places" will have different values and opportunities; and it shows in their prices.

Twenty-four ounces of Coca-Cola or Pepsi on a shelf in a supermarket cost a lot less than they do at a lunch counter in the same store.

#4 Activity Based Costing (ABC)

One of the positive developments of ECR was the acknowledgment that "going in" gross margin didn't make sense as a means of evaluating an item's profitability and contribution performance. This lesson, delivered by the alternative formats, is particularly true in today's dynamic markets. Used in manufacturing for many years, the technique of activity-based costing (ABC) has become a way to look at the delivered cost of a product to the consumer. As value is more tightly aligned with processes and practices, "direct margin" begins to take the place of gross margin, at least in theory. (Many practices — cultural organizational, measurement, and trade — still interfere with the implementation of this important concept).

. . .it would be much better if ABC were used to match revenues with value created. . .

Like most ECR efforts, ABC was used to rationalize the logistics processes of the industry. And this is a valid use of ABC. Yet, as I talk about later in the book, it would be much better if ABC were used to match revenues with value created, thereby defining the new economics of the **AGENTRY Model**.

#5 Third-party Logistics

In the United Kingdom, leading retailers are using a third-party logistics company to make sure their customers get the meal solutions they want. Here's how the service works.

Each of the participating retailers offers its customers a ready-to-eat meal — say, chicken curry. Each meal is formulated and branded to meet the expectations of each store's customers; yet, each is prepared by the same third-party commissary, then delivered to the stores by the same third-party logistics company.

The value of this "cooperative" to retailers is that each can offer a unique home meal replacement solution without incurring excessive "kitchen" and logistics costs. Each can offer differentiating, store-branded products, without paying the high price of handling small, perishable products. Each can focus energy on the core competencies that are important: marketing and product development.

The key to success is understanding the economics of third-party logistics. The third-party distributor does not buy and resell the product (any more than Federal Express buys and resells the packages it delivers). Rather, it earns a *distribution* fee for doing something better than the individual retailers can: i.e., *timely and effective logistics.*

The UK retailers know product differentiation is a competitive advantage, but logistics is not. In fact, when it comes to "fashion food," the expense makes self-distribution a competitive *dis*advantage; hence, the willingness to share a distributor for these items. If it works for perishable "fashion foods," which are value-

The UK retailers know product differentiation is a competitive advantage, but logistics is not.

added solutions, wouldn't the same idea be even better for branded products, which are the same in every store?

A recent article in the *New York Times* details the innovative approach of a company that assembles personal computers for many of the major PC manufacturers. Clearly, the assembly function (parallel to the kitchen and logistics function in food retailing) is very important, but not core, to the manufacturers' competitive positioning. In fact, they probably can't do it as well as this "third party". These PC companies are *marketing* personal computers. Wouldn't the same concept make even more sense in food retailing, where a third-party company could store, handle, and move non-differentiating food products, all in support of retailers marketing their stores to targeted customers?

#6 Consumer Direct

In *consumer direct*, the consumer uses technology, not a store, to shop. The time and place of the *transaction* are 100 percent under the shopper's control. In addition, *delivery* occurs when and where the shopper chooses: to the office, to the "fresh" store for pickup, or home. In some ways, this sounds like a "twist" of the basic distribution model of today's industry: the manufacturer creates the market for its products, a distributor (retailer) gets the products to the consumer. The "twist"? *No store!*

The industry is already seeing the beginnings of a *consumer direct* channel with the emergence of service providers such as Peapod, Scotty's or Streamline. Some retailers are innovating here, also; Hannaford, Tesco, Sainsbury, and Price Chopper to name a few.

Through Peapod, shoppers can use their personal computer to order anything from its supermarket partner (in Chicago, Jewel Food Stores). Initially inhibited by the four walls of the conventional store, Peapod now has its own picking centers, the use of which increases the service's efficiency. Yet, because the merchandise itself is still supplied by the retail grocer, some supply-chain, non-value-added activities/costs are still in this model.

The industry is already seeing the beginnings of a consumer direct channel. . .

Five reasons why consumer direct *out of a store* won't work. . .

- Stores are high-priced, inefficient distribution centers with many operating costs not required by consumer direct.
- The "yield pricing" required by a store to cover the rent results in product pricing that is not based on cost to serve. This then results in the false economics of price subsidizing.
- Stores are limited to the assortment they can carry.
- Trade dollars are still part of the economics of a store, yet these marketing dollars cannot be targeted in a store like they can in consumer direct.
- Consumer direct's short lead times allow make-to-order, especially important in prepared foods. Stores need the product available in anticipation of the shoppers, a source of shrink.

Streamline more closely resembles a true *consumer direct* channel because the company picks products out of a 60,000 square foot warehouse (Peapod is now using warehouse picking, too). The store is completely cut out! Streamline delivers once a week to a consumer's unattended locked storage box which accommodates three temperature zones — dry, refrigerated, and frozen. It's been said that loyal customers spend more than $6,000 per year. Streamline has created a natural switching barrier by providing a valuable service: the easy replenishment to the home of core items and other products. Who would switch back to the old (store-based) way of shopping once he or she made the shopping experience conversion and got used to this highly convenient, frictionless process? Yet, while Streamline removes the store from the process, it still buys and resells the product, which makes their approach just as vulnerable to the same "promotions" and "deals" as land-based stores.

> **Streamline has created a natural switching barrier by providing a valuable service. . .**

Just how big is the opportunity of the *consumer direct* channel? To find out, Andersen Consulting worked with leading manufacturers, retailers, wholesalers, and *consumer direct* companies to research the likely acceptance of PC/Internet based consumer direct shopping in the food industry.

The study interviewed more than 1,800 U.S. consumers to determine their attitude, behavior, and expectations toward the *consumer direct* delivery of products and services. It also compared the purchasing behavior and decision making of 800 consumers currently using a form of *consumer direct* with those of shoppers in the traditional retail channels. (True to SMART STORE™'s mission, it kept in touch with consumer goals and attitudes.)

As part of this effort, consumers were segmented according to their likely acceptance of the *consumer direct* channel, using that perspective to shape a vision of how companies might make more of the *consumer direct* opportunity. What did the researchers find out? Stated simply: *consumer direct* could grow to an $85 billion channel by 2007. The reason why is apparent: *Consumer direct satisfies emerging consumer lifestyle needs.* In a recent presentation delivered at the 1998 GMA Executive Conference, Jeff Levy, CEO of Relevant Knowledge, Inc., predicted that by 2000, the number of U.S. households buying groceries on-line would jump to nearly seven million homes (versus 10,000 in 1997). In fact, groceries will be among the top four e-commerce categories by the end of the century. In its July 20, 1998 issue, *Time* (citing Jupiter Communications) ranks the grocery industry no. 3 in on-line revenues, with a total of $270 million in 1998 (for comparison, the No. 1 industry — travel — racked up $2 billion in on-line revenue).

As I've already discussed, consumers' expectations are changing because of significant demographic shifts. More than at any time in the past, consumers are a diverse group; they're a busy group; and they're more demanding. One thing they are beginning to expect is that retailers and manufacturers will help make their lives more manageable, less complicated, and a little easier. (Customer economics have changed considerably, but the basic store has not.) They want the shopping experience to be both *more* entertaining and informative and *less* stressful and fatiguing. (Shopping for the best deal on a core item has none of these qualities). Food retailing has started to meet these new expectations, as is evident in the availability of prepared foods and easy-to-fix meals, as well as consumer direct offerings, in many major supermarkets today.

Consumers are willing to change where and how they shop if changing fulfills a key need. In fact, even though *consumer direct* is in its infancy, this new channel already meets some consumer needs *better* than traditional channels do. It's more convenient and efficient for the shopper. At the same time, it will be more cost-effective for the industry down the road as

Consumers. . . expect. . . retailers and manufacturers will help make their lives more manageable, less complicated, and a little easier.

redundancy and false economics are driven out of the supply chain, especially for the distribution of nationally branded products and of the core items the shopper knows and wants. *Consumer direct* flies in the face of the industry practices of the past 20 years; rather than assuming shoppers will *come to them*, retailers (or someone else) can use neighborhood stores and consumer direct to *go to the busy customer*. That's the future.

10 Marketplace Truths

1. Each store's market is different.

2. Shoppers care only about their *own* stores in their *own* neighborhoods, and they don't care how products get there.

3. Shoppers don't shop one category per trip.

10 Marketplace Truths (continued)

4. National branded products are, by definition, non-differentiating for customers in picking a store.

5. The cashier is more important than the CEO. Shoppers don't know the CEO; neither do store employees. Most organizations today are irrelevant to shoppers and employees

6. A small percentage of shoppers make up a large share of profits; a small number of core items make up a large share of shoppers' annual purchases.

7. Cross-functional teams are a symptom of dysfunctional organizations.

8. The "bigger" the organization, the more information is required to eliminate risks, support consensus, and manage to averages.

9. Today's "best" marketing/merchandising information systems are ineffective; people are a better source for understanding and interpreting the customer.

10. Retailers and manufacturers are measuring the wrong things. Mass marketing dollars are wasted.

SAYING ONE THING and DOING ANOTHER....

Two things every retailer should know . . .

1. When SMART STORE™ started ten years ago, it surveyed the top five executives in the management teams of 90 retailers to find out: *What's important to your business?*

Customer loyalty was the No. 1 response, with 96 percent of the executives saying it was critically important. (Four percent obviously didn't understand the question.)

The close No. 2 response was *maximizing the potential of each store*, with 94 percent saying it was critically important.

Yet, in November 1995 (six years later), *Supermarket News* surveyed the top *marketing* executives in a comparable number of retailing organizations. Their top priority? Getting *promotional dollars* from manufacturers. Tied for last in their priorities were *local store marketing* and *loyalty programs*. This gap between what we say we want and what we actually do in this industry was large ten years ago, four years ago, and yesterday. Little has changed in the past decade!

2. Every time I'm in a workshop with retailers who have both corporate and franchise stores, I always ask, *"Which stores perform better?"* The answer is always the franchise stores. Is it because the franchise owner cares about his store (and only his store) and will, therefore, make the "formula" work to its potential in his market, for his customers? If the store doesn't perform, the owner can't pay his mortgage! Corporate stores and franchise stores have the same products, the same store design, the same logistics infrastructure, etc. The difference between the two is this: franchise owners pay attention to shoppers and appreciate employees as essential to the maintenance of personal relationships with customers; the corporate store manager focuses on promotions (his own - to headquarters!), appropriately so, given that's the route to greater personal income. Is this why most of the innovation in the industry comes from the independents?

Endnotes

8
p. 32
Industry associations could not participate in the study because of potential FTC conflicts. Because of their ECR affiliation, the associations could suggest *efficient* promotions (less paperwork, electronic administration) but not attack the root cause of the problems: *the practices themselves.*

9
p. 35
Food Institute Report, February 8, 1999

10
p. 38
Why couldn't supermarkets do the same thing? If the supermarket had a strong brand identity (for fresh foods or solutions or home meal replacement, for example) and shopper trust, it could offer a limited choice within a core-item category (say only 20 SKUs of detergent), lower the prices on these items, and make more money at the same time, just like the alternative formats.

11
p. 44
A few years ago, Andersen Consulting proved the validity of this statement with an experimental Internet application called *Bargain Finder*, which would search and find the cheapest distributor of any compact disc title. Pricing was not dependent on location. Some interesting questions: *What is the role of the distributor in a virtual world? Why doesn't the producer sell directly?*

12
p. 44
One argument in favor of today's industry model says that competing retailers keep prices down. If two stores — say, Jewel and Dominick's — are in the same neighborhood or even side by side (which happens often enough), their competitive positioning supposedly results in the lowest prices for the shopper. There might be some truth to that. But, let's not forget a few, simple facts: 1) they have to make money, and 2) their costs are, for all practical purposes, equivalent. This means that a lower price for one product means a higher price for another. In this way, the overall "cost" to the shopper is the same. Of course, "price shopping" is problematic for another reason: It's hard work! The shopper's decision is really between Crest and Total toothpaste, not between the Crest from Jewel and the Total from Dominick's. Eliminating price as a differentiator clarifies the value of products and stores, based on their market attributes. That's the level playing field virtual shopping brings about.

13
p. 45
It is interesting to watch the business models of the new virtual retailers unfold. Many of them, such as Amazon.com and Buy.com, are looking to build future revenues and long-term profits based on their marketing asset — loyal shoppers — and not on real assets such as stores or even inventory.

14
p. 50
The industry's two responses to saturation — consolidation and globalization — will only make matters worse. These "release valves" do not address market conditions in home markets; worse yet, they repeat today's mistakes (i.e., mass marketing tactics that no longer work in developed markets) in new markets. Why not use a "clean slate" in these developing markets?

15
p. 50
Today's 17 percent decline in sales per square foot says it all. Yet, each time I speak to groups of retailers I ask, *How many of you are building new stores?* They all raise their hands! Their organizations, measurements, and business practices won't let them do anything else! And it's the same old store. We keep focusing on logistics and scale!

16
p. 56
Another problem with loyalty programs is the use of the shopper's money to create the reward. The customer pays for the food; if the loyalty program is perceived as a pricing gimmick (which most of them are), what is its value? Is the retailer taking the shopper's discretionary money and giving it back as discounts through the loyalty program? Why not offer everyone the same low price, then give the truly loyal customers a reward? Dorothy Lane Stores offers loyal shoppers a price reduction off the top; the amount of the reduction varies by the "loy-

alty" (measured in frequency and volume) of the shopper. The greater the loyalty, the larger the discount. In most cases, airlines did it right. First, the passengers do not buy most airline tickets; companies buy them. So, the perks of frequent flying are truly rewards for all the miles a businessperson logs in airports and airplanes (not for purchasing the ticket). Second, the more one flies the greater the reward. Nonetheless, the fact that all airlines have frequent flyer programs puts them back at the drawing board to find a way to differentiate the flying experience. In other words, even good loyalty programs, *if they're not differentiated* in another way, lose their edge over time.

17
p. 57
In the early years, SMART STORE™ set up a CEO Advisory Board that worked hard to define "quality" in the supermarket industry. After two meetings, they came up with this quite simple and effective definition: "Continually exceeding shoppers' expectations through people." I believe this describes the loyalty process very well. But how are customers actually measured in today's industry? As a $25 transaction.

18
p. 64
Andersen Consulting has documented many success stories, as well as simple methodologies, in a two-volume publication, *Solution Selling I and II* (1997 and 1998), summarizing findings of a study conducted with GMA.

Imagine ...

. . .A marketplace in which products, information, and funds flow freely, without barriers — all seeking their proper use in satisfying shoppers' desires.

. . .A marketplace in which retailers compete on the value of the total shopping experience and manufacturers compete on the value of their products.

. . .A marketplace in which the success and growth of a business are directly related to the loyalty of its customers.

Just such a marketplace — a *Frictionless Marketplace* — is the next phase of the industry, the phase that will see the triumph of marketing productivity.

In a *Frictionless Marketplace*, innovation is highly valued. Power has shifted to the shopper, while technology like the Internet — embedded in everyone's daily lives — drives the economics of an **AGENTRY Model** for the industry.

The Best of the Past; The Best of the Future

What will the next phase of the industry look like? As I've suggested, we're seeing glimpses of it already. Imagine a new industry model that combines the best of the past (such as personal service from an "**AGENT**-like" grocer) with the best of the future (such as labor-saving technologies which make it easy for shoppers to capture a *moment of desire*) to create a *Frictionless Marketplace*. Let's imagine that marketplace, while staying firmly grounded in today's paradigms: today's *shoppers*, today's *economics*, and today's *technology*.

Shoppers: Sophistication and Lifestyles

Today's shoppers are very different from those of 40 years ago when the industry's current model started. Everyone's familiar with these facts: harried working women don't have time to shop or cook, but are willing to spend more on convenience. Overall, food is a relatively smaller part of disposable income. From "microwaves" to McDonald's, lifestyle changes encourage people to postpone the *what's for dinner?* question until the last minute. At the same time, saturation makes shopping more exhausting and less pleasant: too many stores and too many products, just when the shopper wants time-saving simplicity. Stores haven't changed in decades (except to get larger); they're

Stores haven't changed in decades . . . they're still like assembly lines producing a week's groceries or like food warehouses.

EXAMPLES OF LARGE CREATURES *with* TINY BRAINS FACING EXTINCTION:

still like assembly lines producing a week's groceries or like food warehouses. The bigger they get, the less satisfying the shopping experience. On the manufacturer's side, excessive promotional intrusions and exaggerated promises have given rise to a general mistrust among shoppers of product performance and price claims.

Economics: Flat Population Growth in Saturated Markets

... .saturation with no real population increase spells disaster.

Current economics are clear, and also different from those when the industry started. In an industry built around scale and growth, demanded by Wall Street and management alike, saturation with no real population increase spells disaster. Yet, the momentum of habit and past success keeps the current model limping along. Why else would retailers keep adding the same kind of square footage to already overwhelmed markets? And isn't that one reason the sales per square foot keep dropping? And why else would manufacturers spend more and more on trade promotions and advertising, with little or no increase in sales or loyalty or profit to show for it?

THE FALSE PROFITS

The mass marketing logistics model has created false economics which show false profits. As a result, two current measurements are almost meaningless in a saturated marketplace. The first is *growth* (rather than shopper satisfaction and loyalty) through a "push" strategy (rather than a pull strategy). A "push" strategy encourages retailers and manufacturers to use marketing (i.e., loyalty programs or special promotions) to get consumers to "switch" rather than to reward customers who are actually loyal. The second is *market share*, which is meaningful only to Wall Street and top management. Market share does not predict future success because it's meaningless to the individual shopper, who cares only about his or her own store and own shopping experience and own core items. Any company figuring that out could shoot to the front of the pack.

Technology: Welcome to the Future

Obviously, technology has changed substantially in the past 40 years. With the advent of the personal computer, power was put in the hands of individuals (for working, for record keeping, and recently for shopping); technology began to work for the *consumer's* advantage. New technologies — such as the Internet, WebTV, and light pens — embed technology in everyday "lifestyle" appliances.[19] Soon, individuals will have "one-click" access to all the information they want, including information about products and services. Each person's trading area will be the world. Comparison shopping will be instantaneous and effortless. Prices will be driven down to the lowest common denominator. The impact of consumer technology on current industry practices will be enormous.

Experts estimate that 50 percent of the U.S. population already use computers at work; school children start using them in kindergarden. Soon-to-be-developed "disposable" computer chips will increase the uses for "computers" dramatically. For example, products will be "smart" with chips in them to facilitate automatic replenishment to the home. PC shopping and light pen scanning will be part of every household, enabling "one-click" ordering and "one-click" loyalty.

All of this is a real challenge to the land-based retailer and, more importantly, to today's industry model. In fact, the importance of the Internet (and other technologies) to the creation

The impact of consumer technology on current industry practices will be enormous.

of a *Frictionless Marketplace* is so great I'd like to spend a bit more time on it here.

The Internet: Bill Gates is betting his business on it. Where does that leave the rest of us?

Bill Gates . . . emphasized the impact the Internet will have on the industry, and on Microsoft.

When Bill Gates spent several hours at SMART STORE™ in 1996, and when I heard him address the CIES Annual Congress in Vancouver, he emphasized the impact the Internet will have on the industry, and on Microsoft. Since then, he has done several key things, among them: 1) purchased WebTV in an effort to bring Internet technologies to consumers' homes inexpensively; 2) entered into agreements with the manufacturers of both televisions and cable set-top boxes to include a scaled-down version of Windows™; 3) purchased Hotmail to secure 15 million eMail subscribers; 4) invested in Firefly, software which anticipates individuals' preferences; and 5) invested in Nextel, for wireless Internet access.

To me, the Internet will be the centerpiece in how individuals get things done — including shopping — in the future. In a recent issue of Andersen Consulting's magazine, *Outlook* (1998, No. 1), Rudy Puryear (Andersen Consulting's partner in charge of its eCommerce practice) explains the impact: "We are moving away from producing for a mass market. We are moving away from marketing through mass communications toward customizing products [and services] for individuals with whom we must build one-to-one relationships. Supply push is becoming demand pull. Indeed, more than 80 percent of companies in the Fortune 500 now have a presence on the World Wide Web, compared to 35 percent just a year ago."

As Nicholas Negroponte wrote in his famous work, *Being Digital* (1995), "Computing is not about computers anymore. It is about living." We're talking about grocery shopping, *yes*. But we're also talking about advertising and fine art, magazine publishing and political campaigning, family relationships and education — *everything!*"

In their recent book, *Unleashing the Killer App*, Larry Downes and Chunka Mui describe the history of technology as one of dramatic and unexpected consequences. They cite examples of inventions — the arch, the pulley, the compass, eyeglasses, moveable type, the steam engine, the cotton gin, asphalt, the Model T, elevators, structural steel, and the atomic bomb — whose impact extended far beyond their inventors' original visions. As a result, the "havoc they visited on social, political, and economic systems has outweighed ... their intended usage."

The same is true of the Internet. It took the world a long time (relatively) to get "wired" for electricity. The adoption of Internet access is happening (relatively) in a blink. Radio existed 38 years before 50 million people tuned in; television took 13 years to reach that benchmark. Once it was opened to the public, the Internet crossed the 50-million mark in four years.[20] Some experts believe that by the year 2000, more than one billion people will use the Internet[21] and by 2002, businesses will use it to conduct more than $300 billion worth of commerce.[22] 3Com's next version of the Palm Pilot™ will have a wireless interface to the Internet for a $10 per month access fee; the company expects to sell one billion in 10 years.

> Once it was opened to the public, the Internet crossed the 50-million mark in four years.

> *"The world now runs on Internet time."*
> ANDREW GROVE
> Chief Executive Officer, Intel

Who's using the Internet? A recent article in The *Public Perspective* summarizes the results of a two-year study: "Once heavily overbalanced by male users, the Web is now accessed by men and women almost equally. And, once predominantly white, the Web population now reflects a racial breakdown statistically indistinguishable from U.S. Census data for the general population."[23] Yet, one distinction did pop out in this research: Americans aged 18-24 — only 13 percent of the general population — account for 21 percent of the Web-user population. Project their buying power over the next ten years! And more importantly, project their attitudes about grocery shopping and preparing food. It is significantly different then their parents.

In 1998, Andersen Consulting[24] conducted a study which set the record straight by showing that the appeal for consumer direct services (via the Internet or similar channels) cuts across all income and educational levels, age groups, and locations. Similarly, a recent study conducted by *Wired Magazine* and Merrill Lynch describes the "Digital Citizen" in terms of personality qualities (such as optimistic, tolerant, civic-minded, and radically committed to change) rather than demographic characteristics.

Commercial Interest. In general, the business world and economic community appreciate the transformational power of the Internet. Entire industries are making the development of Internet customer relationships a core strategy. (Many Internet retailers do not plan to make their profits on traditional product gross margins; they plan to make their money by leveraging their marketing asset, loyal customers.) In fact, lots of companies and individuals are making a real commitment to the Internet as an important channel for business.

For example, the Vice President of Marketing for Procter & Gamble, Denis Beausejour, recently announced the $35.8 billion consumer products company is doubling the number of brands it advertises on-line, while calling for a "Summer Summit" with Coca-Cola, Levi Strauss, McDonald's, AT&T, and other major advertisers to "figure out what it will take to transform the Web into the space it can be."[25]

. . .the appeal for consumer direct services. . .cuts across all income and educational levels, age groups, and locations.

HEY! THIS IS GREAT! WE SHOULD BE DOING BUSINESS IN HERE!

In the summer of 1998, Unilever announced a three-year interactive marketing agreement with America Online, the single-largest commitment to the Internet channel by any packaged goods manufacturer. As many as 100 Unilever brands — from cleaning and personal care products to foods and beverages — will benefit from a prominent presence throughout AOL, with a focus on popular and contextually relevant areas such as cooking, entertainment, health & fitness, childcare, cosmetics, and toiletries.

Tesco, the United Kingdom's largest supermarket chain, has signaled its understanding of the power of the Internet. In addition to its consumer direct offering — one of the industry's best — the company is now morphing itself by becoming an Internet Service Provider. The retailer wants to be **the** portal to the Internet: What incredible exposure that would create for its Web page! How easy that would make virtual shopping! Each time a user logged onto the Internet, he or she would have the option of beginning, continuing, or completing the grocery shopping, with access to an expanded line of products and services.

The retailer wants to be the portal to the Internet. . .

By purchasing TCI for $31.7 billion in stock, AT&T hopes to become the Internet conduit to America's homes. Similarly,

NBC has purchased a 60 percent share of Snap, CNET's Web portal. And CBS purchased SportsLine.com for $100 million. Why? Because more Americans are getting their news from Internet sources. In 1997, Intelliquest reported, "PointCast released results of a survey verifying that 46 percent of Internet users are reading fewer newspapers, 23 percent are reading fewer magazines, and 21 percent are watching less television." According to Relevant Knowledge, a leading Internet research company, in early 1998 the top five-visited Web sites (#1 Yahoo; #2 Netscape; #3 Micr osoft; #4 Excite; and #5 Infoseek) had a larger audience than the top five-viewed television programs (#1 ER; #2 Seinfeld; #3 Suddenly Susan; #4 Friends; and #5 The Naked Truth).

Last, but not least — anyone can open a store on Yahoo! or on many other services in less than 10 minutes and for a minimal amount per month (a small "slotting allowance" or "trade promotion expense"). They provide the software, on-line access and payments processing; the business or individual provides the products and services. Instant access to a market of millions! (Case in point, this book can be purchased through **www.AgentryAgenda.com**.)

> *"New entrants, unencumbered by a long history in the industry, can often more easily perceive the potential for a new way of competing. Unlike incumbents, newcomers can be more flexible because they face no trade-offs with their existing activities."*
>
> MICHAEL PORTER, *Harvard Business Review*

From a recent press release... America Online Inc. (NYSE:AOL), the world's leading Internet on-line services company, and NetGrocer, the first nationwide on-line supermarket on the World Wide Web, announced an agreement making NetGrocer the exclusive on-line supermarket shopping delivery service on AOL and AOL.COM.

NetGrocer will make its nationwide service available to AOL's more than 11 million U.S. members...[letting] shoppers across the United States purchase non-perishable supermarket items on-line at competitive prices. Brand name products are available in categories including groceries, pet care, health and beauty and housewares.

A variety of lower priced brands are also available. NetGrocer is the first and only on-line supermarket to cover cities, towns and rural areas nationwide and charges no membership fees. All transactions are secured by the latest on-line secure socket layer technology.

"We expect NetGrocer's offerings to be a big hit with our convenience-minded audience," said Bob Pittman, AOL's president and COO.

Business Wire

No Time to Trek to Tai Tam for Some Kangaroo Tail at Market Republic? Several Hong Kong supermarkets now offer convenient virtual shopping, so you can enjoy browsing the aisles 24 hours a day and avoid bumping into the Saturday afternoon masses. Ordering is easy, delivery is cheaper than a taxi ride, and the services are reliable...The sites also offer the same specials and prices as in the supermarkets.

...The Parknshop cyberstore, which was launched in May, is the

continued next page

Tai Tam (continued)

most comprehensive of the on-line grocers with more than 4,000 items, including fresh meats, fish and vegetables. . .The Parknshop site is easy enough for even technophobes to conquer. You click on a list of departments, like bakery or fresh foods, or look at a labeled floor plan of an actual store and click on the section you want. Then you click on the desired item to put it in your virtual basket. The screen shows a running total of how much you have spent, and shoppers can save lists of items they buy regularly for easier selection next time. Registration and check out are fast, and you can pay with Visa, American Express or cash upon delivery. . .If you order before noon, Parknshop will deliver the same day within a specified window of time.

> *Asian Wall Street Journal,* as reported by Individual, an on-line news service. Edited for inclusion here.

"If only ten percent of consumers choose to purchase half their grocery needs on-line within three years, that would pull five percent, or $23 billion, in retail sales from the brick-and-mortar grocery universe. (This assumes total supermarket and other food store sales of $460 billion annually, based on U.S. Department of Commerce figures.) This is a conservative estimate, since the profile of active Internet shoppers tends toward upscale, time-pressed, dual-income families - not coincidentally the same profile as most supermarkets' heaviest buying customers. ... How many currently operating supermarkets could sustain the loss of five to ten percent of their volume and still remain viable? In an era of over-stored markets, what percentage of supermarkets already operates on the brink?"

> JAMES TENSER, editor and publisher of *VStoreNews,* the electronic newsletter for the emerging virtual retailing industry, writing in *Sales & Marketing Quarterly* (Summer 1998).

The economics of the Internet. . .

- The fastest growing categories of Web users are females ages 12-17 (55 percent) and females 50+ (42 percent).

- Nearly 77 percent of all Web users are between the ages of 18 and 49.

- Just over 50 percent of Web users are college graduates, compared to 24 percent of the U.S. population.

- Almost all college students use the Internet in their studies; 50 percent of employees in the U.S. use the PC in their daily work.

- Nearly 50 percent of users visit five or fewer sites per day.

- Eighty percent of users go to only one site to buy books;

- 92 percent go to only one site to buy CDs.

- By the year 2000, 69 million people in the U.S. will buy goods via the World Wide Web; the total spent via e-commerce will equal $26.8 billion.

- When every television is Web-enabled, "surfing" the Net will be as easy as watching NBC is today.

- The convergence of telecommunications and the information technology will embed the ability to shop virtually into every-day appliances, such as relatively inexpensive WebTV or lights pens.

Source: JEFF LEVY, Relevant Knowledge, Inc. and various other sources

The Microsoft Corporation recently partnered with key vendors, such as Barnes and Noble, promising them exclusive business if they put their "catalogs" on Microsoft's Intranet. Each employee was given a $1000 purchasing authority. Now, an employee can buy an item (from an approved vendor) on-line just by clicking and pointing; the vendor delivers the goods directly to the employee. The company has cut the cost of purchasing transactions by $1.6 million annually.

(Source: 1998 ANDERSEN CONSULTING LEADERSHIP COUNCIL)

Dell Computer is growing at four times the market rate. The reason? Using an enlightened e-commerce presence to invite customers to "build your own computer on-line." The more than 10 million visitors to Dell's Web site in the fiscal quarter ending 2/1/98 also had immediate access to a broad array of customer services, including 45,000 pages of technical support data. Special "Premier Pages" are set aside for its biggest customers. In 1996, Dell sold $1 billion worth of computers (90 percent to business customers).

Source: *Outlook*, 1998, No.1

Does Amazon.com live up to its hype? YES

Each and every article written about e-commerce includes at least a mention of Amazon.com, that Internet phenomenon. Since opening its virtual "storefront" in 1995, Amazon.com has shipped books to 1.5 million customers worldwide. Among these, the company enjoys a loyalty rate of about 80 percent, according to a profile of Jeff Bezos, founder of Amazon.com, in a recent issue of *GQ* (March 1998).

The same article describes Amazon.com as a "front," taking orders on its Web site, then purchasing the books from the warehouses of big wholesalers and publishers. When Barnes & Noble and Borders opened up their virtual stores, many industry analysts expected Amazon.com to be crushed. But it wasn't. One reason might be Amazon.com has signed up 30,000 "affiliate" Web sites that recommend books and link to the site for a commission on sales.

Also, Amazon.com notifies customers of new titles in their areas of interest (see the facing page for a copy of an e-mail I recently received), as well as encouraging readers to submit reviews and build up a small, personal stake in the company's success. This one-to-one, *value-added* merchandising and loyalty building is real! And it works. Amazon.com has built a community of customers, and these customers keep coming back. Why go anywhere else when the "shopping experience" at Amazon.com is so good? Being "first" — and being really good at what it does — this company has created a real switching barrier. What would motivate a customer to go to the trouble of "teaching" a new vendor?[26] Relevant Knowledge has confirmed this loyalty to be as high as 85 percent. No wonder Amazon.com is reinvesting much of its revenue in attracting and keeping customers.

In July, 1998, Amazon.com enjoyed a market capitalization greater than that of Barnes & Noble and Borders combined. But it trailed both companies in sales for the first quarter of 1998: Barnes & Noble, $666.3 million; The Borders Group, $545.3 million; Amazon.com, $87 million. Still, not bad for a company that is only four years old and that has forced its two huge competitors to open up Web sites of their own. The market maintains its enthusiasm; while shares of Barnes & Noble gained 34.3 percent in the six weeks beginning June 1, 1998, shares of Amazon.com were up more than 179 percent for the same period.

Relevant Knowledge has confirmed this loyalty to be as high as 85 percent.

> It took Sam
> Walton 12 years
> to break $150
> million;
> Amazon.com has
> done it in three!

Flush with success and recognizing the potential profitability in leverage (especially potent because the company is not inhibited by brick-and-mortar assets), Amazon.com is now going after the markets for music and videos, changing its advertising tag from "world's largest book store" to "books, CDs and more." Consumer packaged goods might not be far behind: Kleiner Perkins Caufield & Byers, the undisputed venture capital firm and backer of Amazon.com, has announced a new venture — Drugstore.com — and everyone is waiting for an announcement of a tie between the two brands. Clearly, investors value the potential of strong customer relationships. It took Sam Walton 12 years to break $150 million; Amazon.com has done it in three!

Dear Mr. Terbeek:

On behalf of everyone here at Amazon.com, I'd like to thank you for ordering from us in the last few months. To put it simply, Amazon.com wouldn't be Amazon.com without customers like you.

If you are like me, you are constantly trying to find good ways to identify your next great read. We think we might be able to help.

Because Amazon.com is blessed with such a large community of book lovers, we can often recommend other books you might enjoy by comparing your purchases to those of other members of our community. While acknowledging that these recommendations may not be perfect (after all, we've only known you for a short time), customers keep telling us our suggestions are helping them find new favorites.

So here are some books we recommend for your next read:

"Grocery Revolution : The New Focus on the Consumer", Barbara E. Kahn, Leigh McAlister
http://www.amazon.com/exec/obidos/ISBN=0673998800

"Cases in Retailing : Operational Perspectives", Cathy Hart, Malcolm Kirkup, Diane Preston, Paul Walley, Mohammed Rafiq
http://www.amazon.com/exec/obidos/ISBN=0631201734

"Competing With the Retail Giants : How to Survive in the New Retail Landscape (National Retail Federation)", Kenneth E. Stone
http://www.amazon.com/exec/obidos/ISBN=0471054429

"Retail Power Plays : From Trading to Brand Leadership : Strategies for Building Retail Brand Value", Andrew Wileman, Michael Jary
http://www.amazon.com/exec/obidos/ISBN=0814793312

"Retailing", Dale M. Lewison
http://www.amazon.com/exec/obidos/ISBN=0134614275

For more personalized recommendations and other ways to discover works you haven't read, but might enjoy, check out our Recommendation Center:
http://www.amazon.com/recommendation-center

Thanks again for your support and for being an Amazon.com customer. Happy reading!

Sincerely,
Jeff Bezos, Founder & CEO
Amazon.com

What Does Everyone Want?

Given these three current paradigms — shoppers, economics, and technology — let's ask three fundamental questions that must be addressed to create the *Frictionless Marketplace*:

What do shoppers want?

Over the last ten years, SMART STORE™, spent a lot of

time finding out what shoppers want. Shoppers were interviewed in stores; they were surveyed on the telephone, and they participated in focus groups in both the U.S. and Europe. In many cases, shoppers were invited to SMART STORE™ to test their reactions to the *Frictionless Marketplace*.

What were the results?[27] Among other things, shoppers want *convenience* (easy access to the products they want). They value meal *solutions* (and other types of solutions) and *information* about new products, meal planning, and nutrition. They'd like it to be *easier* to shop, and they like stores that are *entertaining*. They want *fair* prices (but will not sacrifice quality to get low prices; in fact, price is important only when a store has no other way to differentiate its offerings).[28] Most important, they want *control* and *answers*. Given an average of 3,000 promotional intrusions per day and more than one million items for sale in a saturated industry, shoppers want help cutting through the process of satisfying their needs.

Most important, shoppers want control and answers.

Another lesson learned at SMART STORE™: Innovation in the industry comes from independents, not because they're small, but because they take the time to talk to their customers. In larger, public chains, store employees often have a good idea of what shoppers want, but their knowledge (a great source for shopper research) is not leveraged by management. All in all, most consumer research goes to headquarters analysts who are not close enough to the shoppers to interpret it correctly or are not willing to take a risk in changing the way things are done even if the research suggests change is right. Change is hard when scale is large. I always tell manufacturers, *"You get your volume at the big retailers, but you get your innovation at the independents!"*

Change is hard when scale is large.

What do manufacturers want?

Ideally, manufacturers want full access to all targeted consumers and information about those consumers. The more

WHAT MANUFACTURERS WANT...

In other words,
shoppers want
barrier-free
access to
manufacturers, and
manufacturers want
barrier-free access
to shoppers.

direct this access, the better. Also, good manufacturers want their products to compete fairly, on their true market value. They want an effective way to introduce and promote new products, including low-cost distribution (sounds like ECR?). Yet, the mass marketing, land-based industry model promotes expensive redundancy, and false economics: lots of stores, in lots of places, all carrying the same items, with lots of marketing dollars spent on the process — everything creating higher and higher barriers. As the number of items in the marketplace increases, mass redundancy makes even less sense. In fact under these conditions, many manufacturers would love to "go around" retailers if they could.

What should retailers want?

How can a retailer make its store the "store of choice" as often as possible? Clearly, retailers should want a loyal customer base. They should want to be able to fulfill their customers' demand for any nationally branded products, all the time and any time. And they should want to create switching barriers (pretty much impossible to do if price is the only weapon in the armory). The retailer needs to compete on a differentiating shopping experience and value creation; success in doing so is measured in long-term customer loyalty. In a market of flat population growth, loyalty is the only way to assure an equal or better volume of sales over time. So, what retailers really want (or need) is the shopper's trust because loyalty equals wealth.

The next phase of the industry will see participants struggling to satisfying these desires. To do so will require change far beyond the incremental improvements suggested by ECR. Rather, the *Frictionless Marketplace* will represent nothing less than a radical departure from our current logistics-driven industry model.

The Principles of a *Frictionless Marketplace*

Given current *shoppers* (sophistication and lifestyles), industry economics (flat population growth in saturated markets), and technology (everything from the Internet to WebTV, integrated into the lifestyle of the consumer), what will the next phase of the industry — the *Frictionless Marketplace* — need to achieve?

Match Revenues with Value Created

This is probably the most important of the principles, because in the *Frictionless Marketplace* the "value chain" is much more important than the supply chain. If a retailer or manufacturer does not provide value as *defined by the shopper*, the company will not be able to grow (or perhaps even survive).

The shopper has power. Any intermediate buying and reselling of products, without adding value to them (i.e., without transforming them or making them part of a "solution"), will not exist long term because the shopper does not value these activities. This is especially true as these activities only *increase* costs. Internet commerce will expose these false economics and drives prices to the *lowest* common denominator.

Value can be created by grouping products into solutions, adding information, providing answers for the shopper, and making shopping itself easy, convenient, social, and fun. Remember, distribution's only value is that it connects the consumer to a product; a "distribution fee" is most logical in this case. Gross margin is not.

Eliminate All Barriers

Nothing should separate shoppers from the products and services they want and need. Today's barriers — logistics, store location and size, industry business practices, measurements, scale, and trade promotions — only support false economics that will not hold up in the virtual world.

Minimize Industry Conflicts

To make the marketplace frictionless, retailers and manufacturers will work together to satisfy the shopper's needs. For example, they'll match the marketing attributes of a retailer's customers to the marketing attributes of a manufacturer's products to encourage shopper loyalty and increase sales with each loyal cus-

tomer. Because of two trends (a flat population and a shift in power to the shopper) this is where retailers and manufacturers will spend their energy — together — if they hope to grow: Loyalty, one shopper at a time!

Level the Playing Field

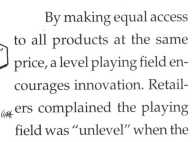

By making equal access to all products at the same price, a level playing field encourages innovation. Retailers complained the playing field was "unlevel" when the alternative formats stole core items from the supermarkets. But these brands are no longer the reason a shopper chooses a store; in the *Frictionless Marketplace*, the store will be valued and successful only because of the value added shopping experience it provides. No more subsidizing poor performing products or products with low prices due to saturation! No more blocking of innovative new items because they can't buy their way into the market. Retailers and manufacturers of all sizes will be able to compete on true market values. Retailers will want to have equal access to all products; manufacturers will want them to have it, too! For sure that is what the shoppers want!

Encourage Innovation and its Rapid, Interpretive Rollout

In the *Frictionless Marketplace*, innovation will be the primary competitive advantage. Innovative shopping experiences and products will win the loyalty (and increased business) of individual shoppers. Land and scale (large size) will no longer be a prerequisite for profit. But employees "in the field" (retailers' and manufacturers') will be *very* important in establishing personal relationships with targeted customers, as well as serving as a source of information about shoppers' lifestyle-based preferences. New ideas will have to roll out quickly in a chain, while each store

will need the freedom to interpret them (and modify them) for use in its own local market. Innovation can be a scale opportunity. Because manufacturers and distributors will need the ability to quickly pick up consumer trends in one area and match them to other markets with the same consumer segment characteristics.

Build Real Loyalty to Retailers and Brands

When the population is not increasing, long-term growth in sales or profit (for a store or a product) comes from the loyalty of each customer. As discussed on page 58, a loyal customer is a profitable customer. Loyalty is the key to marketing productivity for three reasons: 1) it costs less to keep a loyal customer or to sell more to a loyal customer than to acquire a new customer; 2) it's easier to anticipate and fulfill the needs of a shopper who is well-known, thereby enabling targeted and successful innovation. Real loyalty cannot be bought; it needs to be earned; and 3) once loyalty is earned, the customer relationship can be leveraged to new products and services.

But there's another reason for loyalty. All over the world, the retailers and manufacturers with the most loyalty also have the highest market capitalization. The obvious example is Coca-Cola. But for another example, just look at the wealth created by good independents and the prices for which they are selling their businesses! Most Internet retailers' strategies are built around this concept, because they cannot compete on price.

Align Organizations, Measurements and Core Competencies with Consumer Values

Today's industry is aligned around product distribution. ECR and cross-functional teams added sophistication, but did not change the underlying logistics bias of the model. (In fact, cross-functional teams, in and of themselves, point to the need for a realignment of our organizations, because the need for them says that our current organizations are functional silos and, therefore, dysfunctional.)

In the *Frictionless Marketplace,* retailers will align their organizations, measurements, and core competencies around the shopping experience (actual and virtual); manufacturers will align theirs around serving retailers, customer-by-customer, store-by-store. The employees close to the shoppers will be the key source of information for both retailers and manufacturers. Many of today's measurements, such as market share, will be irrelevant, unless it's the share of a targeted household's food expenditures. Long-term loyalty will be more important than short-term sales increases.

Build a Platform for Growth

All companies need growth; it's a sign of success respected by (and even demanded by) customers, employees, and investors alike. But definition of "growth" will change from "gain in scale, size, and power" to "increase loyalty and innovation by keeping employees close to shoppers and sharing knowledge across the organization." With this type of growth, profits will follow because marketing productivity will dominate and drive logistics productivity — a lesson we should have learned from the alternative formats.

Achieve ECR Objectives

One of the minimum requirements of the *Frictionless Marketplace* is that it meets the objectives of ECR. Above and beyond delivering a potential $30 billion in savings to the industry, ECR was meant to achieve efficient *assortments*, efficient *replenishment*, efficient *new item introductions* and efficient *promotions*. I agree: these objectives are important to the industry *and* shoppers. How can you argue with them? In fact, they are fundamental. The very idea of "frictionless" implies maximum efficiency — maximum efficiency in marketing that will drive maximum efficiency in logistics. I believe the *Frictionless Marketplace* will achieve efficiencies much greater than ECR hoped to achieve because it will align the whole industry around the shopper's needs and the two processes to achieve them: *Demand-side* and *Supply-side*. This will eliminate the current barriers that prevented ECR from achieving its objectives.

The Moment of Desire; The Moment of Value

The fundamental promise of a *Frictionless Marketplace* is twofold: 1) it makes possible the easy capture of a shopper's *moment of desire*; and 2) it empowers the shopper to close the gap between a *moment of desire* and a *moment of value*. These achievements will increase marketing productivity substantially.

Right now, an individual might have a *moment of desire* — for a meal, for a party idea, for nutritional information, for a recipe, for a tube of toothpaste. The desire can be created in many ways; for example, by an advertisement, by a display in a store, or by the need to replenish a favorite product when it runs out. Today, to capture that *moment of desire* (and turn it into a *moment of value*), the individual needs to go to a store. That barrier won't exist in the *Frictionless Marketplace.* Today, the retailer controls *when*, and *how*, and *where* the individual shopper satisfies his needs and desires. Tomorrow, the customer will have that control. Remember, technology will put the ultimate power in the hands of the shopper.

Today, the retailer controls when, and how, and where the individual shopper satisfies his needs and desires. Tomorrow, the customer will have that control.

The 9 Principles of AGENTRY AGENDA™

1 Match Revenues with Value Created

2 Eliminate All Barriers

3 Minimize Industry Conflicts

4 Level the Playing Field

5 Encourage Innovation and its Rapid, Interpretive Rollout

6 Build Real Loyalty to Retailers and Brands

7 Align Organizations, Measurements and Core Compentencies with Consumer Value

8 Build a Platform for Growth

9 Achieve ECR Objectives

For years, the fashion industry has tried to do a more efficient job of capturing shoppers' *moments of desire* by using catalogs to bring merchandise into the targeted customer's home. (But it's still selective mass marketing, at best). From a catalog, a shopper can make a purchasing choice *whenever* and *wherever* it happens to be convenient: the reader sees, decides, buys — from the comfort of her home. The customer has more control. Yet, some variables are still out of her control, such as the day/date the catalog is delivered to her home. And, of course, the catalog is at least somewhat out-of-date by the time it's being used. Hence, electronic commerce — which is 100 percent under the control of the shopper and 100 percent up-to-date — could eventually eliminate catalog shopping for the same reasons it could make today's supermarket obsolete.

The significance of *consumer direct* companies and Internet shopping is that they enable the shopper to capture and satisfy a *moment of desire* without the store; the store is no longer a barrier to access because the store is no longer in the picture. The capture of the *moment of desire* and conversion of it into a *moment of value* are opportunities for huge marketing productivity gains. To gain an appreciation of just how huge, look at the redemption rate of coupons. How much greater would it be if shoppers could scan coupons with a light pen at home at the time they decide they want the item? Or "click on" to buy a product being advertised by using the remote to their WebTV?

When it comes to a food *moment of value* — i.e., the consumption of food — restaurants obviously have grocery stores beat hands down. In the past, that didn't matter because supermarkets did not realize they were competing with restaurants (and other immediate *moment of value* satisfiers — everything from McDonald's to vending machines). Now, that's not the case anymore. Hence, we see more and more retailers selling prepared meals and even opening up "grills" or "lunch counters" or "salad bars" in the store itself. Why was this missed by the *Alternative Format Study?*

Finally, one significant aspect of the *moment of value* concept is this: the "fair price" of a product or service changes as the individual gets closer to the *moment of value*. A hot dog from a vendor at a baseball game costs ten times as much as a hot dog in a package in the supermarket. A glass of wine in a restaurant costs almost as much as a whole bottle in the liquor store. Coke in the soft drink section is much cheaper than the Coke in the supermarket's deli. Why? Because in each case, the products are ready to be consumed the exact moment the individual wants to consume them.

> The capture of the *moment of desire* and conversion of it into a *moment of value* are opportunities for huge marketing productivity gains.

Moment of Value. . .In Action

- eatZi's — an 8,000 sq. ft. "store" in Dallas developed by a restaurant giant, Brinker International — bridges the gap between supermarkets and restaurants by offering products from both, including masterfully merchandised fresh prepared entrees, salads, and bakery along with limited grocery items such as beverages and snacks. Twelve chefs staff the flagship store at all times, and the dinner hour routinely causes traffic jams in the parking lot. The company has opened (or is opening) stores in Houston, Atlanta, New York (17,000 square feet in the basement of Macy's), Long Island, and Maryland. According to *Progressive Grocer* (August 1998), executives are considering sites in Boston, San Diego, and Plano, Texas.

- McDonald's is partnering with convenience stores, gas stations, food and non-food retail stores — all attempts to expand the fast-food giant's accessibility at the consumer's *moment of value*. One would expect McDonald's to embrace this strategy simply because this fast-food leader (and the fast-food industry itself) played a large role in redefining the consumer's *moment of value* for eating as immediate (fast!), convenient, predictable, and affordable.

- Kraft Foods has opened the Hot Dog Construction Co., exclusively showcasing Kraft's line of Oscar Mayer products in the Atlanta airport, and has plans to open formats featuring other Kraft brands such as DiGiorno Pasta and Rich's baked goods. These position Kraft as a "solution provider" that can directly meet the needs of busy and hungry travelers.

- Marks & Spencer in the United Kingdom has been tremendously successful with a line of ready-to-eat entrees and sandwiches, as well as with its Sandwich Stores. Ukrop's Super Markets (based in Richmond, Virginia) has takeout meals (Dinner for Two™), salad bars, and in-store grills and sit-down eating areas. Sainsbury's, another UK retailer, has branded its in-store restaurants so strongly that people come to the store *first* to eat, then to shop. Perhaps the next step here would be a stand-alone, sit-down restaurant.

When Starbucks opened hundreds of little boutiques — each one near its customers' *moments of value* — where were the "center-of-the-store" coffee manufacturers of the industry? Starbucks — a company which really understands its consumers — is perhaps the best example of competing by meeting the individual's *moment of value*. First, the company branded a concept, *Starbucks equals gourmet coffee*, at the same time, creating *desire* for a niche item. It put tiny stores all over the place, in every nook and cranny where its consumers are. It developed a direct mail channel, including a coffee of the month club, and a virtual store. Then, Starbucks put kiosks in airports and bettered that channel by becoming the exclusive coffee provider on United Airlines flights. For its ingenuity, Starbucks gets better margins and the ability to reach its target consumers in yet another time and place — at yet another *moment of value*. (All of this has been accomplished with virtually no "consumer research." To keep innovating in response to customer preferences, Starbucks tries a new idea in a store; if it's popular, it's rolled out to other stores.)

The Next Logical Step

Technology creates an efficient way to capture a *moment of desire* and/or satisfy a *moment of value*. Consider the remarkable success of automated teller machines (ATMs) and of on-line banking from home. At first, people were anxious about conducting transactions without a teller; now, who can imagine giving up the convenience of ATMs? Through ATMs, we withdraw cash, deposit checks, or transfer balances just about anywhere, 24 hours a day. Just as interesting, ATMs are completely non-differentiating (as is the "product" they distribute): every bank has them; and customers can access their accounts from any ATM, even those sponsored by other banks. With PC banking, location is not an issue at all; banking can be done from home, night or day.

Despite the "commodity" nature of ATMs, technology can bind a customer to a bank. For example, automatic payroll depositing and automatic bill payment increase the hassle of switching to another bank. For Nationwide Building Society (a Savings and Loan) in London, Andersen Consulting built a kiosk which allows a customer to look up his stock portfolios or, find out the performance of his investments, as example. The customer can also "click on" access to a real banker (the contact is visual through cameras), who sees at a glance the same screens the customer has been reviewing; the real banker answers questions, provides additional information, or even suggests other products/services to buy. (Demonstrated at SMART STORE™ Europe.)

The technology-enabled banker is like an **AGENT**, managing many transactions for the customer, keeping the customer informed of his account status, paying the customer's bills, and suggesting new financial instruments which might be appealing based on the banker's understanding of the customer's financial holdings and plans. In fact, the next logical step for banks would be to leverage this **AGENT** role to sell other products or services in much the same way a company like Amway offers a catalog of products above and beyond its "core" items.[29] And remember, all banks are supported by a "market level" clearing house — in the U.S., it's the Federal Reserve Bank — to make their "**AGENTRY Model**" work.

One premise behind the *Frictionless Marketplace* is the growing comfort people have with the Internet and other technologies. As these technologies become embedded in our lives — through WebTV, for example — *access* to products and services will be even more constant, immediate, and convenient for the shopper. In fact, the shopper will *need* the retailer (acting as an **AGENT**) to capture various *moments of desire* — 24 hours a day, seven days a week.

See a product advertised on TV; click YES on the remote; the item is added to a virtual shopping list maintained by an **AGENT** (*your* **AGENT**). Run out of toothpaste; use a light pen to scan the tube before throwing it out; the item is added to the same virtual shopping list. Read an ad in a magazine; use the light pen to scan the bar code at the bottom; the product is on the list. The *moment of desire* is captured automatically and instantaneously. And, when the shopper indicates, the *moment of value* is satisfied through delivery of the completed list at the individual's convenience and choice (whether to the home or to a pickup location).

After the War, Albert Heijn built his business by just about giving away new technology — small refrigerators, in fact — counting on the fact that, with the right "appliance," people would buy more groceries from his store. He was also enabling the success of the newly emerging mass marketing industry model. He was right, of course.

Why wouldn't a retailer choose to support today's newly emerging *Frictionless Marketplace* (made possible through an **AGENTRY Model**)? Wouldn't it make sense for today's retailer to give away an equivalent technology — say light pens or WebTVs — with which the shopper could order products from his or her own kitchen by scanning the bar code? (Remember, IRI gave away POS to start their business, FreePC.com is giving away PCs to start their business). Just think of the switching barrier that would create! Today's logistics-based model will topple, once and for all.

Endnotes

19   In its new business plan, Microsoft's primary
p. 81   focus is on the convergence of computers and
other information and entertainment sources,
such as the television and telephone.

20   Ibid. page 4-4. In 1989, the World Wide Web
p. 83   (WWW) protocols for transferring hypertext via
the Internet were first used in experimental form
at the European Center for Particle Research
(CERN) in Switzerland. In 1991, the National
Science Foundation lifted the restrictions on the
commercial use of the Internet. That same year,
the WWW was released by CERN. In 1993, the
alpha version of Mosaic, the graphical user interface to the WWW, was released, giving non-
technical users the ability to navigate to the
Internet. This report uses 1993 as the date when
the Internet became truly open to the public.
See: Cerf, Vint. "The Internet Phenomenon."
National Science Foundation web page. http:/
/www.cise.nsf.gov/general/compsci/net/
cerf.html.

21   "The Third Shall Be First: The Net leverages
p. 83   latecomers in the developing world." *Wired
Magazine*; Nicholas Negroponte; January 1998.

22   Op cit. U.S. Department of Commerce; 1998;
p. 83   page 7-7; and Forrester Research.

23   "Web Users Are Looking More Like
p. 84   America." *The Public Perspective*, April/May
1998; pp. 33-34.

24   Along with the Consumer Direct Cooperative
p. 84

25   "The IQ Q&A: Denis Beausejour, Procter &
p. 84   Gamble explains why the Web will be The
Biggest Medium since TV". *IQ Magazine*;
Michael Schrage; July 20, 1998.

26   When I first bought Quicken™ software, it sat
p. 91   on the shelf for about six months. Finally, I took
the time to load it up, figure out how to use it,
put in all my financial data, etc. Now, I don't
know how I ever lived without it! Would I

bother to replace Quicken™ with a different
product? Of course not! Why would I go to all
that trouble? What would be the advantage?

27   One thing learned is that traditional shop-
p. 94   per research is not always reliable because it
often presupposes today's store. For example, *What's your favorite part of the store?* It
should allow the customer to express his or
her true desires. Like, *What would be the best
imaginable ways to get groceries into your kitchen
or to prepare dinner?* Like the rest of us, shoppers relate best to what they already know.

The research at SMART STORE™, on the other
hand, was not prescriptive; rather, it's open-
ended. And the results are often amazing. For
example, when considering the hassle of buying staples (often nationally branded products that shoppers find both trustworthy and
predictable, hence not requiring "touch and
sight" to buy), one elderly British woman
actually said: *"I bet these basic items could be
kept in a warehouse and delivered to my house
cheaper than through a store."* That's one of the
clearest expressions of the value of a virtual
channel for food I've ever heard.

28   At the CIES Marketing Forum in Berlin sev-
p. 94   eral years ago, retailers and manufacturers
were asked to cite the reasons a shopper se-
lects a store. The "top two" responses were
price and *assortment* — clearly, answers expected from a mass marketing audience. Yet,
in a different survey that same year, European
shoppers ranked *price* and *assortment* #5 and
#6 on their list. Other reasons that were more
important included freshness of produce,
friendliness of staff, cleanliness, and location.

29   Amway provides its shoppers a number of
p. 109   "core items" that can be replenished easily,
even automatically. In addition, customers can
choose from a catalog of about 7,000 additional
branded items. The trust that Amway customers have for the company because of their
individual, personal **AGENT** translates into
comfort of buying non-core items as well.

4 ▪ THE AGENTRY MODEL

agent: (ā ′jent) 1) One with the power or authority to act. 2) A means or mode by which something is done or caused. 3) **A retailer that has earned the right to anticipate and deliver goods and services which fulfill the needs and expectations of individual shoppers, whether through a virtual or actual store, because of relationships built on trust.**

CORE ITEMS' ROLE

Enables:

Supermarkets	**1945**
Alternative Formats	**1975**
Consumer Direct	**1995**
AGENTRY	**2000**

The purpose of an **AGENT** is to make things happen. In this industry, the "things" that have to happen include: 1) anticipating and delivering value to the shopper by providing answers and control; 2) creating and capturing a shopper's *moment of desire* to benefit both the shopper and the manufacturer; 3) resolving uncertainty by providing ready access to information and solutions; and 4) making it easy to restock kitchen shelves with staples, as defined by each shopper's household.

What does it mean to be an **AGENT**?

In the *Frictionless Marketplace*, there's little to prevent the customer from capturing his *moment of desire* and satisfying his *moment of value*. This near-perfect commerce is brought about through a new model — the **AGENTRY Model** — which returns in spirit to the relationship-centered values of the Pre-Development phase.

An **AGENT** (like "mom and pop") looks out for the best

This near-perfect commerce is brought about through a new model — the AGENTRY Model. . .

interests of its customers and brings to its *own* shoppers the right "stuff" — the right goods and services, based on the **AGENT'S** informed, deep understanding of the shopper's desires and preferences. The **AGENT** creates value by anticipating the total needs of local shoppers; capturing their *moments of desire* whenever and wherever they occur; fulfilling their expectations; and satisfying their *moments of value* through two stores (the best of the past and the best of the future):

THE RIGHT STUFF

- an *actual* store, where customers find meal solutions, prepared foods and fresh foods, as well as information and social contact/entertainment. In fact, in the *Frictionless Marketplace*, actual stores will be able to exist only if they create value through solutions, convenience, excitement, etc. In the actual store, the shopper will also find a modest assortment of staples (core items) — just enough to satisfy the local market's need for "quick trip" items and convenience. I call this the *moment of value* store.

- a *virtual* store, through which the shopper easily replenishes any core item (products used all the time in the shopper's household), other nationally branded products,

In fact, in the *Frictionless Marketplace,* actual stores will be able to exist only if they create value. . .

113

or even perishables once trust is established. A virtual store can also provide value-added solutions through the bundling of products and/or services, through information such as recipes, and through "chat rooms" or other forms of two-way communication.

With a full view of his or her shopping activities, the **AGENT** can meet all the customer's needs — from full meal replacement solutions to the replenishment of staples and packaged goods. In fact, the "stuff" the **AGENT** delivers does not have to be limited to food or products sold in today's stores. Once a consumer direct infratsructure is created that's robust enough to move large-bulk, low-value-per-pound food items continuously to the home, **AGENTS** can leverage this infrastructure to deliver just about any product (videos, flowers, electronics, recipes) or service (dry cleaning, banking), as long as customers believe in the **AGENT'S** quality and efficiency.[30] This would be an opportunity for growth unique to the food industry.[31]

The idea of **AGENTRY** means capturing the shopper's *moment of desire*, then delivering products or services to create the *moment of value*. Like fashion retailers who use "personal shoppers" for their best customers, an **AGENT** knows all about a customer's preferences; the **AGENT** could suggest complementary merchandise, and the shopper would trust the **AGENT'S** recommendations. Nordstrom has grown in tight markets because of its **AGENTRY**-like personal service.

> This would be an opportunity for growth unique to the food industry.

How does the **AGENTRY Model** Work?

The **AGENT** 1) anticipates the shopper's needs for solutions and information; 2) captures the shopper's *moments of desire*, however they are created; and 3) makes sure the shopper has easy access to any and all national branded products. This is done through both actual and virtual stores.

AGENTRY MODEL

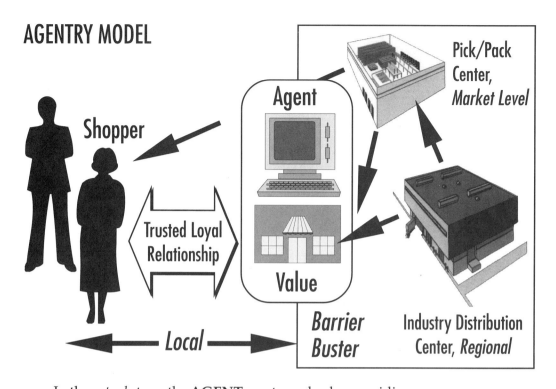

In the *actual* store, the **AGENT** creates value by providing answers (*What's for dinner tonight? What new products would make sense in my kids' lunch? What's an easy-to-prepare menu for brunch for 12?*), convenience and of course a neighborhood shopping experience. Through a *virtual* store, the **AGENT** makes possible the delivery of any other product not carried in the actual store. The replenishment of core items is done with as little effort as possible on the shopper's part.

The **manufacturer** puts any and all products in centralized regional warehouses managed by a *Barrier Buster,* who makes these products available to all **AGENTS** (and, thereby, all shoppers) at the manufacturer established cost. The independent *Barrier Buster* creates the most efficient logistics system by driving redundancy and false economics out of the supply chain.

Manufacturers pay the *Barrier Buster* a standard fee for inventory management and distribution. Any manufacturer can put product into the warehouse; small, new companies would

> The independent *Barrier Buster* creates the most efficient logistics system. . .

have the same *physical* access to shoppers that large manufacturers do. If they can create *moment of desire* (through advertising or through the **AGENT**), they can compete effectively. Likewise, smaller **AGENTS** will be able to compete effectively, since the "muscle" of today's large land-based chains will disappear.

Manufacturers will find many more ways to create *moments of desire*. For example, a manufacturer posts a recipe on its Web page; by clicking, the customer downloads the recipe and adds its ingredients to her virtual shopping list being maintained by her **AGENT**. The **AGENT** delivers the ingredients with the shopper's next scheduled delivery.

. . .the "muscle" of today's large land-based chains will disappear.

ACTUAL
SHOPPER

VIRTUAL
SHOPPER'S
PROFILE

The Economics of the **AGENTRY** Model

The **AGENT'S** two stores — actual and virtual — are complementary and synergistic. However, the business processes and systems behind them are different to be true to the principles of the *Frictionless Marketplace*. Together, the stores form a shopping experience continuum:

- A good *actual* store experience can increase the shopper's trust and loyalty, thereby encouraging and supporting the use of the **AGENT'S** virtual channel.

- A good *virtual* shopping experience can create a barrier that decreases the likelihood of the shopper switching to another retailer. The virtual "store" creates a "one-click" loyalty in customers that can transfer to the actual store: Why use another resource once the connection and shopper knowledge is established?

For an **AGENT** to compete on the shopping experience continuum, it will need a "shopping profile" of each customer that includes products ordered virtually as well as in the actual store. Obviously, each customer will shop the continuum differently.

THE **AGENTRY** TRIANGLE

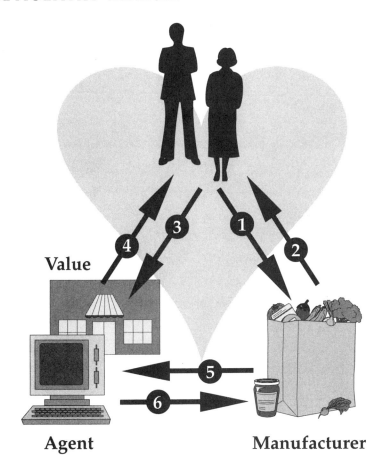

Value

Agent

Manufacturer

1. Shoppers want barrier-free access to core items and innovative products.

2. Manufacturers want barrier-free access to shoppers.

3. Shoppers need **AGENTS** to create and capture the *moment of desire* and create a good shopping experience (a *moment of value*).

4. **AGENTS** need loyal shoppers to stay in business.

5. Manufacturers need **AGENTS** to capture shoppers' *moments of desire* for their products.

6. **AGENTS** need manufacturers to create *moments of desire* for the core items and innovative products that shoppers want.

Loyalty and Technology Converge The following two stories (edited here) appeared nearly side-by-side in CIES' *Food Business News*, September 1998. The first cites a study first reported in the *Harvard Business Review* (July-August 1998), the second a study conducted by AC Nielsen.

E-Commerce: A boost to retailer loyalty

U.S. - The Internet is likely to boost repeat shopping of certain types of products that consumers are already familiar with ... The study suggests that retailers of "experience products" [those that consumers are willing to buy over the Internet only as repeat purchases once they have bought them in a physical store] should view their physical stores as a channel for building relationships with customers, while using the Internet as a cheap way to handle repeat orders.

Warning: loyalty cards can reduce loyalty

U.K. - Many consumers are shopping around more as they learn to take advantage of the financial benefits of loyalty cards. As a result, loyalty cards are now having the opposite of their intended effect ... Unsurprisingly, consumers with multiple cards are up to 20 percent less loyal to any single store ... loyal shoppers perceive the cards as being little more than gimmicks ... There is also little evidence that, in a market saturated with loyalty programmes, the cards are helping to boost retailers' market share.

This mix of "stores" and shopping experiences makes for a greater return on investment, return on differentiated space, *and* return on loyal shoppers. The **AGENT** knows his customers — what they like and dislike; what they want and don't want — and adjusts the shopping experiences (actual and virtual) accordingly. Intimacy and flexibility represent a shift from

programs designed to encourage switching — a Saturation
phase tactic — to programs designed to encourage loyalty.

COMPELLING ECONOMICS (26.5% margin or 10% distribution fee?)

	Traditional Store	Pickup Point
Sales/wk.	$300,000	$300,000
Sq. Ft.	40,000	23,000
Ctr. Str. Sales/wk.	$150,000	$150,000
Ctr. Str. sq. ft.	20,000	3,000
Margin	(26.5%) 39,750	(10%) 15,000
Labor	(10%) (15,000)	(4%) (6,000)
Inventory Cost	(1,000)	—
Direct Margin	$23,750	$9,000
DM/sq.ft.	$1.19	$3.00

Consumer Direct
Economic Impact

Perhaps the *actual* store stocks ten different wines — five
that are appropriate table wine for the local market, and five that
are part of a home meal replacement solution. This selection varies by week, depending on meal solutions being offered in the
store, other specialty foods being offered in the store (say, cheeses
from France), and the focus of the monthly meeting of the store's
wine-tasting club. All other wines — say, 500 different types —
are readily available on request through the *virtual* store (as is,
perhaps, an on-line link to a California winery or a chatroom
like *Wine News*). The **AGENT** presents wine as part of a "value-

added" program, making all other wine alternatives available via *consumer direct*. Why let "Virtual Vineyards" have this business? By the way, isn't this a very efficient (ECR) assortment?

Or the store might carry a small selection of laundry products recommended as a complete laundry solution, along with a part-time laundry expert for problem consultation. All other detergents are available virtually; the laundry expert is available through a virtual link on the shopper's Internet site or through an in-store kiosk, like ones being tested in the Albert Heijn stores in the Netherlands. (These kiosks work similarly to those created by Andersen Consulting for Nationwide Building Society) In fact, the **AGENT** is not just an aggregator of products like today's retailer; rather, it's also an aggregator of experts. This suggests opportunities for **AGENT**/manufacturer alliances.

In the **AGENT'S** organization, store employees are a critically important source of information, just as they were in the Pre-Development phase. While POS can record what sells, only employees can relate customer reactions and inquiries, which are much more important in selling solutions profitably. They'll be encouraged to engage shoppers and suggest improvements based on what they find out about shoppers' objectives. Labor in the store moves from below the value line to above the value line because the smaller store requires far less inventory handling and stocking-type activities and far more interaction and involvement with shoppers.

AGENTS and manufacturers focus all their attention on working together to match the market attributes of individual customers to the market attributes of individual products. They find innovative ways to increase shopper satisfaction and loyalty by sharing data gathered about buying patterns and by planning ways to improve the local market performance of each store. In the Frictionless phase, today's cost-of-product time consuming issues disappear.

Labor in the store moves from below the value line to above the value line. . .

In the Frictionless phase, today's cost-of-product time consuming issues disappear.

In the *Frictionless Marketplace*, the manufacturer sets the *virtual* selling price and has more overall control of the product's market performance. Due to our saturated markets, there is more then enough product competition to encourage manufacturers to keep prices competitive. Advertising (direct mail, Sunday supplement, television, etc.) creates a *moment of desire* for the product; the shopper "asks" the **AGENT** to find/deliver the product, for example, by scanning the bar code on the print ad or touching the TV remote. The **AGENT** gets the branded product from an independent, centralized distributor — a *Barrier Buster* whose job is moving product, information, and money efficiently through the entire supply chain. The *Barrier Buster* frees manufacturers and **AGENTS** to put their energy into competing for the shoppers' loyalty by satisfying all aspects of the *moment of value*. The manufacturer *creates* demand for branded products; the **AGENT** *fulfills* demand through the virtual channel, without buying and re-selling products. And everyone is rewarded according to the value they create. The **AGENT** doesn't care what the shopper orders virtually; it only cares about maintaining the shopper's loyalty by fulfilling the order as expected.

The **AGENT** can also create demand for branded products in the store by including them in *solutions*, or simply by carrying them if they think they are important to their shoppers to have in the store. Once the product is in the actual store (and manufacturers can certainly suggest value-added promotions that include their product; for example, *New Healthy Breakfasts for Kids!*), the risk and rewards for product performance are the **AGENT'S**. If the *wrong* product (i.e., one not valued by the local customers) is in the store, or if a solution is unsatisfactory, the **AGENT** takes the hit. The value of an **AGENT** diminishes in their shoppers' mind, if this happens often. For this reason, the **AGENT** pays for an item as it enters the store and controls its use from that point on. And that's the way it should be. This is why I don't

In the *Frictionless Marketplace*, the manufacturer sets the virtual selling price and has more overall control of the product's market performance.

Once the product is in the actual store. . . the risk and rewards for product performance are the AGENT'S.

like scan based trading. It implies that the manufacturer has some "ownership rights" over the merchandising in the store since they in effect own the product. But it is the **AGENT'S** job to create the shopping experience, not the manufacturers, other then through "selling" the marketing attributes of their products or solutions to the **AGENT**.

RETAILERS DESIGNING THE SHOPPING EXPERIENCE

> The backbone of the AGENTRY Model is the idea that payments for products. . .occurs when value is created and/or when risks are taken. . .

Matching revenue to value: Where does the buck stop?

The backbone of the **AGENTRY Model** is the idea that payments for products (or the transfer of ownership) occurs when value is created and/or when risks are taken — an idea very foreign to the way this industry does business, especially since saturation set in. But this idea is very important in trying to match revenues with value, thereby taking false economics out of the system.

When markets were not saturated (the Pre-Development and early Development phases), and when there were (for all practical purposes) no branded products, retailers provided value by picking and assembling products for the shopper. And they took risks with the unbranded products themselves. *Was the butter good?* But in today's markets, the retailer adds no value (other than distribution value) by buying and reselling nationally branded products as they are, unless they are bundled in solutions or are available for an immediate *moment of value.* What difference does it make where the shopper buys their favorite brand? The desired product is exactly the same everywhere. In fact, that's the strength of a national brand. Finding a brand on sale (if that's a priority) is simply a hassle; it creates a negative shopping experience and, potentially, undermines brand loyalty for both retailer and manufacturer.

The **AGENTRY Model** matches the revenues generated with the value created. For example, in the actual store, the **AGENT** takes the risk of carrying the wrong products (since the small store can't carry *all* products) or by not having the right items. Wonder if the local shoppers don't like the store's selection? They'll go elsewhere. The **AGENT**, therefore, assumes real marketing risks. For these reasons, the **AGENT** pays when the product enters the store (it's owned by the manufacturer until that point). By creating a *moment of value* in the store and taking the associated risk, the **AGENT** earns the right to charge what they want for the products. The shopper will always have the opportunity to buy the same product virtually and, in fact, use the virtual price point (set by manufacturers) for comparison. So, the **AGENT** will need to be careful to align the price

. . .in today's markets, the retailer adds no value. . . by buying and reselling nationally branded products as they are. . .

123

in the actual store with the value created by carrying it in the store. This will really drive efficient (ECR) assortments.

In the virtual channel, **AGENTS** want to get the shoppers any items they want; failure to do so will diminish the value the **AGENT** delivers. Manufacturers create *moment of desire* for the product and set the product's price. Remember, with comparative shopping made easy by the Internet, prices will fall to the lowest common denominator.[32] For products purchased virtually, the **AGENT** receives a standard activity-based distribution fee. The performance measures for the virtual store would likely include order completeness, on-time delivery, expertise in selecting the appropriate perishables, innovation in building products to create a "new" solution, ease in capturing the customer's *moment of desire*, etc.

AGENTS can create added value in the virtual store, too — perhaps by providing information, or creating *moments of desire* for private label products, or bundling products and/or services into solutions. In these cases, the **AGENT** creates a value-added "new" product and can price it accordingly. If the solution includes nationally branded products, the **AGENT** receives *both* the standard distribution fee for each item and the premium that can be charged for taking additional risks in creating the solution.

In actual stores, promotional dollars are paid at the time the shopper buys the product. Again, this payment reflects real value created and real performance. (Of course, a good **AGENT** will not promote items inappropriate for its own, local shoppers regardless of promotional moneys because that would reduce the trust between them.) Let's say an **AGENT** uses the actual store to introduce a new product. After a while, the product would join those available through the virtual store unless the **AGENT** can find a *new* reason for it to be valuable to shoppers in the actual store. For example, it could become a quick-

For products purchased virtually, the AGENT receives a standard activity-based distribution fee.

trip convenience item, or part of a new solution, or featured periodically to stimulate impulse purchases.

The *Barrier Buster* — breaking down barriers between manufacturers, **AGENTS**, and customers — receives a distribution fee (just like FedEx or UPS) also determined by activity-based costing (ABC)[33]. If the manufacturer wants to put an item in a market, it does so by paying the *Barrier Buster* a fee to handle the inventory. The manufacturer owns the product until it goes to the actual store, at which time the transfer price of the product is charged to the **AGENT**. For a virtual sale, the value equal to the manufacturer's set retail price, less the **AGENT'S** and the *Barrier Buster*'s fees, is transferred to the manufacturer. The *Barrier Buster* also creates/gathers timely information about shopper segments and store segments that would be given to the manufacturer as a by-product of doing business. Extra analysis of data might incur an additional charge.

WHICH LOGISTICS SYSTEM IS BETTER?

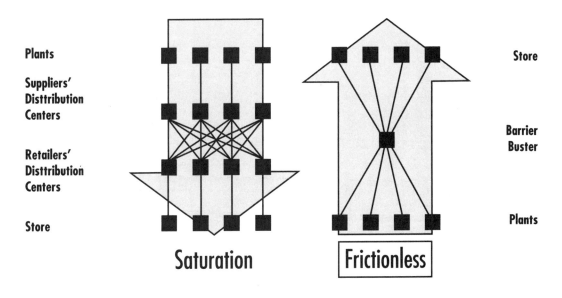

A few years ago, I was taking a taxi to a Wegmans store in Rochester, New York. Making small talk with the driver (not a man of means), I asked where he shopped for groceries. *"Wegmans."* Why, I asked. *"The people are so friendly. The fresh food and prepared meals are great. I love the shop. I enjoy being in the store."* Do you ever shop anywhere else, I asked. *"Once or twice I tried another store, but I always come back to Wegmans."* After a slight and thoughtful pause. *"You know, Wegmans does charge a penny or two more on some items, but so what?"*

The **AGENTRY Model** rewards any business that does one of two things well: gives consumers more value (in stores, in products, in service delivery); or cuts waste and cost out of the supply chain by expediting the movement of products, information, and funds. (It can't do both without compromising results). A new business is able to realize its potential based on the value it brings rather than on its size.

NEW BUSINESSES WILL REALIZE THEIR
POTENTIAL BASED ON THE VALUE IT
BRINGS INSTEAD OF ITS SIZE

The AGENTRY Model. . .

For AGENTS. . .

.it means providing the best shopping experience, whether through new formats, solution selling, private label, more value-added services, *consumer direct* virtual channels, and many other innovations.

For manufacturers. . .

.it means enabling products to succeed on their value through better access to consumers; the effective capture of *moments of desire* created through advertising; new "partnerships" with retailers; low-cost distribution; and many other innovations.

For shoppers. . .

.it means an **AGENT** is helping by providing convenient, easy access to all products; information and solutions designed to meet immediate and intimate *moments of value*; convenience and control over the shopping experience.

For *Barrier Busters*. . .

.it means the opportunity to create the new generation "logistics network" unimpeded by any false economics caused by the misalignment of revenues, organizations, and measurements with the shopper's value.

AGENTRY Model turns the industry on its head ...

SHOPPER'S CHOICE

150
Shopper's Core Items

AGENT

1,000,000
Items in the Market

AGENTRY MARKETING

In a market the size of Chicago, there are approximately 500 supermarkets, each one carrying 40,000 items, most of them redundant. That's 20 million SKU points! The typical shopper buys 150 core items which make up a large percentage of his or her annual purchases.

In the *Frictionless Marketplace*, it's economically sound to have twice as many stores, each one smaller and closer to the marketplace (the *moment of value*), each one carrying 5,000 items (or only five million SKU points) appropriate for the local market. This works out to potentially one-fourth the "SKU points" in today's marketplace, yet with a much better overall focus on the needs of the individual. The space available to core items versus value items will change dramatically, since core items will most likely be delivered consumer direct. Just think two small stores in the same market area as one old large store and each could have a unique market proposition, young professionals for one, young families for the other.

Inventory and storage/handling costs in the store are radically reduced. At the same time, the shopper is able to procure an additional 100,000 items or even more — in fact, *any* product the manufacturer decides to put into the market — through the *Barrier Buster*. The six retailers' and wholesalers' warehouses in Chicago today, plus the many manufacturers' warehouses, would be consolidated into one.

The individual customer has *more* access to *more* products without being inconvenienced or overwhelmed by the chaotic and stressful choice of today's crowded, mass market store. The **AGENT** provides more product to its customer, with, one could argue, as little as one-eighth the inventory in the store and one-fourth the inventory in the market.

The **AGENTRY Model** makes possible (truly and for the first time) the realization of the four objectives of ECR and of the *Frictionless Marketplace*: Efficient assortment, Efficient replenishment, Efficient promotions, and Efficient new item introductions. The *Barrier Buster* can achieve true logistics economies because redundancy is removed and the false economics of "push" marketing are eliminated.

More about the *Barrier Buster*

The *Barrier Buster* does just what its name says: *busts* barriers between shoppers, **AGENTS**, and manufacturers, while (at the same time) improving the efficiencies and leveling the playing field of the whole system, to the benefit of everyone — especially the shopper. In fact, the *Barrier Buster* is nothing less than the most important player in the *Frictionless Marketplace*.

First, let's talk about what the *Barrier Buster* is *not*. It's not an outsourcer for logistics because that would be yet another attempt to "clean up" the old system.[34] It's not market level logistics,[35] since it does much more by introducing the business practices and economic incentives which encourage manufacturers and retailers to *work together*.

What is the *Barrier Buster*? A real breakthrough — a new way of thinking — the enabler that makes possible the *matching of revenues with value created and the aligning of product marketing attributes with shoppers' desires and expectations*.

In short, the *Barrier Buster* creates the *Frictionless Marketplace* — frictionless from the shopper's perspective, from the manufacturer's perspective, and from the **AGENT'S** perspective. Products, information, and funds flow in the most efficient manner. The competitive playing field is level, with companies vying to create true consumer value.

In fact, the *Frictionless Marketplace* encourages competition because it 1) reduces the capital required to get in the game for **AGENTS** and manufacturers, and 2) enables *any* item, no matter how small or particular,[36] to reach its target customers and compete based on its market value. This sounds exactly like what shoppers want: companies targeting their needs, capturing *moments of desire* and satisfying *moments of value* through a fulfillment system much, much cheaper than today's.

> The *Barrier Buster* does just what its name says: busts barriers between shoppers, AGENTS, and manufacturers. . .

The *Barrier Buster* is responsible for the flow of three things in the *Frictionless Marketplace*:

- *Products*. The *Barrier Buster* creates a single inventory system with 100 percent product visibility. No more pockets of inventory in the wrong place; no more confusion about where a product is and who's responsible for it.

  The *Barrier Buster* helps to manage product-specific inventory in the regional warehouses and the pick/pack centers in line with market needs, keeping in mind two things: 1) **AGENT**-driven store promotions and products use in solutions (once the product inventory is in the store, the **AGENT** manages it); and 2) the level of sales through the virtual channel (which would be influenced by manufacturer controlled pricing, "special offers," and advertising.) Today's problems — out-of-stocks, forward buying and diverting, unsaleables, redundant warehousing — go away.

- *Information*. Information is an important by-product of the *Barrier Buster*'s activities. For example, manufacturers get timely information about the real market performance of products, segmented by actual stores, virtual stores, shopper demographics, and the source that created the *moment of value*. Just think of the power they'll have to influence sales through *real-time marketing*. If market share for a product is too low or if a customer segment is underperforming, the manufacturer can lower its price in the virtual channel; run ads focusing on a target segment that isn't responding as positively as predicted; or work with an **AGENT** to promote the product in a solution in the actual store, after showing how the product will appeal to that store's local shoppers. Just compare how trade dollars are spent today with the productivity of *real-time marketing*. The benefits are obvious!

Just compare how trade dollars are spent today with the productivity of real-time marketing.

131

By providing **AGENTS** and manufacturers data — such as product sales by store or by customer segment or by "source of desire creation" — the *Barrier Buster* helps them match the marketing attributes of the product to the desires of individual shoppers, thereby enabling the continuous improvement of both store and product marketing performance. This is particularly important, because in the *Frictionless Marketplace*, revenues are matched to value created. Both parties are rewarded for marketing precision, and mistakes could be costly. The industry will gain the power (real-time information!) to move from mass marketing to one-to-one marketing.

Wouldn't it be nice if discussions between trading partners were based on marketing attributes, rather than on costs, invoice deductions, unsaleables, and other logistics-based issues?

For example, a manufacturer might put a new product in the market, but does not (or cannot) create a desire for it. This product marketing failure would be expensive. Similarly, if an **AGENT** puts a product in its store or suggests it to a shopper virtually, but the product isn't accepted by the **AGENT**'s shoppers, the risk of losing a customer's business is greater. (Wouldn't it be nice if discussions between trading partners were based on marketing attributes, rather than on costs, invoice deductions, unsaleables, and other logistics-based issues?)

The *Barrier Buster* enables the **AGENT** and manufacturer to work together to increase shopper loyalty to both the store and the product. Obviously, an **AGENT** competing for the long-term loyalty of the targeted shopper will not — and should not — share with the manufacturer the identity of a specific shopper because the **AGENT** owns the relationship. But, through the *Barrier Buster*, the **AGENT** will share customer segmentation data, because the manufacturer can help the **AGENT** decide which products make sense in which stores or for which shoppers. Also, if an

AGENT can prove an anonymous shopper is loyal to both the store and a product, probably a core item, the manufacturer might give that shopper a special loyalty price through that **AGENT** only. If the loyalty is broken in either case, the special treatment is discontinued. Imagine! Relevant marketing! Loyalty marketing! Growth in flat markets!

Finally, the *Barrier Buster* provides, at a standard cost, common information in a data warehouse for use by the industry, including basic item data, costs, marketing attributes, etc.

- *Funds*. The *Barrier Buster* becomes the clearing house for the industry. Who needs the hassle of managing payables and receivables, anyway? Since the *Barrier Buster* ships to each store for the manufacturer, and since the store takes ownership of the inventory when it's received, it only makes sense that the *Barrier Buster* act as the go-between in the transfer of funds from the **AGENT** to the manufacturer (less the amount due to the *Barrier Buster* for logistics activities). Of course, controls and audits would maintain the integrity of the system. A once-a-week transfer statement would be very economical. Just imagine: The issues of invoice inaccuracies — Gone! If it works it the banking industry, why not in the food industry?

The *Barrier Buster* becomes the clearing house for the industry.

If the **AGENT** and manufacturer agree to an in-store promotion, then (true to the *Frictionless Marketplace*) the allowance dollars would be paid based on actual **AGENT** performance; i.e., when the product is sold. Remember, the **AGENT** will choose to feature a promotion store by store based on its value to local shoppers. The payment of the allowance dollars would be included in the weekly transfer-of-funds statement. Doesn't this sound much easier than the going in gross margin computation which is so very out of touch with market reality anyway? The **AGENT'S** accounting is simpler and to the point. Finally, activity-based costing is much easier for **AGENTS** in the *Frictionless Marketplace* because they have only store activities to consider. In effect, the total store will be DSD through one source — the *Barrier Buster*. Once more, the store will be a marketing value center, with fewer, more targeted items and more service.

Similarly for virtual sales, the *Barrier Buster* transfers the proceeds the manufacturer earned at the time the order is under the control of the **AGENT**. This fee is the manufacturer's set retail price, less the **AGENT'S** and *Barrier Buster*'s fees. The *Barrier Buster* also credits the **AGENT** with the distribution fees earned for delivering the nationally branded products. Any premiums charged for solutions will stay with the **AGENT** since they created the added value. In the case of private label, the **AGENT** is both retailer and manufacturer, taking risks similar to those of manufacturers and earning revenues for the value created with the private label. Private label and national brands will compete on the same playing field through the *Barrier Buster*.

Who will be the *Barrier Buster*?

To be successful, and to ensure a *Frictionless Marketplace*, the *Barrier Buster* must be completely independent of **AGENTS** and manufacturers; otherwise, the temptation to build barriers (rather than bust 'em) would be too great. Also, the services provided by the *Barrier Buster* must, by definition, be limited to prevent any conflict of interest.

First, the industry associations such as FMI, GMA, CIES, FDI and others should form an alliance to focus on the principles for the **AGENTRY Model** and provide oversight of the **AGENTRY Model** as it forms. ECR was supported by these

First, the industry associations. . . should form an alliance to focus on the principles for the AGENTRY Model and provide oversight of the AGENTRY Model as it forms.

groups and did do a good job in getting the industry to work together; maybe the same joint effort would work here. (Why spend time cleaning up the old model when that effort can be spent instead on the new model? Wouldn't that make more sense?) One of the alliance's responsibilities would be to select the administrator and other service providers for the *Barrier Buster* network. Organizations already in place could make the transition easy.

Organizations already in place could make the transition easy.

A likely candidate as the overall administrator of the *Barrier Buster* service could be the UCC (Universal Code Council) or the EAN (European Article Number) Council, since by assigning UPCs and EANs they already oversee an industry-wide, trusted practice. There is no advantage in redundancy in this area, just as there would be no advantage in redundancy in the Federal Reserve Bank. The UCC or EAN could outsource by markets exclusive rights for the logistics and information-processing activities of the *Barrier Buster*, while establishing standards of performance for the franchise. Potential candidates for outsourcing would include: 1) third-party logistic companies already operating, particularly in Europe; 2) today's wholesalers if they could divest their retail interests, 3) information services companies that already have the networks in place; and 4) large-scale system integrators with the capacity to build and execute the information systems. Service providers would be paid a standard activity-based transaction fee.

Most likely, the *Barrier Buster* would be a *network* of service providers[37] under the control of the administrator. This would be required because: 1) the size of the operation is large, and one company probably couldn't operate it all effectively (nor would the industry want one company to operate all of it), 2) if designed properly, the network could provide contingency backup to cover other nodes, and 3) competition would keep the competitive spirit alive.

Most likely, the Barrier Buster would be a network of service providers. . .

For example, the regional warehouse (or information processor) in Chicago and the one in Detroit might be managed by different companies; so might the frozen foods and grocery logistics within the same region. In such cases, the benefit of separate management would be the ability to benchmark best practices and continuously improve performance through peer competition. This network approach already works in many industries. In the transportation industry, for example, a national airline might control the reservation system but outsource commuter operations to regional airlines that are more focused and cost-effective. Several airlines already outsource the "clearing" of airline tickets to Andersen Consulting.

Finally, remember: the *Barrier Busters* — whoever's running the show — will be professionals whose core competence is logistics or information processing. The *Barrier Buster*'s *only* focus will be improving efficiencies in its area of expertise. The model will not let marketing dollars degrade performance the way they do now. The industry will benefit from having an *integrated* information and distribution network; no more worries about creating unique interfaces with each trading partner.

At a CIES logistics conference in Europe a couple of years ago, both retailers and manufacturers complained about the complexity of one-to-many interfaces growing out of cross-functional teaming. (However, Marks & Spencer, because of its 100 percent private label business, was able to say, *if you want to do business with us, you have to use our system*.) The *Barrier Buster* concept saves everyone from the one-to-many headache. Wouldn't it make more sense to spend time working together than to spend it trying to connect?

> Wouldn't it make more sense to spend time working together than to spend it trying to connect?

Is Any U.S. Retailer Following the AGENTRY AGENDA™ Today?

I think Dorothy Lane in Dayton, Ohio comes close. The actual store — not much bigger than 15,000 square feet in a middle-class neighborhood — makes the best of what many would think of as limited space. The store has plenty of solutions; prepared meals, in-store chefs, a great bakery (famous for "Killer Brownies"), its own Starbucks-like coffee bar, great meat and fish, a floral department, and on and on and on. Then, in the traditional center-store categories, Dorothy Lane favors variety over redundancy in its merchandising. I saw only three plain yellow mustard SKUs — the two most popular brands, one in two sizes — simple! (How many would a national chain store have?) And for variety, one each of several specialty mustards.

Following AGENTRY AGENDA™ (continued) Employees like working in the store; as merchants, they show appropriate pride and "ownership" of their areas. The shoppers appear to be very loyal. Even before implementing a loyalty program (and Dorothy Lane has one of the simplest, but also most progressive, programs in the industry), the store manager would call 15 shoppers per day to ask them about their shopping experience. More recently, shoppers are rewarded for buying; the more one shops, the more one saves.

No wonder Dorothy Lane is a great place to shop. The people are friendly; the store is manageable; the differentiation is unique. Also, management is located in one of two stores, not distracted by logistics and other non-store issues. Anticipating the needs of shoppers is not a research project, it is part of management's daily activity.

Dorothy Lane also has a fun, interactive Web site, where customers can order their signature food items (those "Killer Brownies" again!), find out about interesting happenings in the community, sign up for cooking classes, etc. The only thing Dorothy Lane is missing — to be a "perfect" **AGENT** in today's marketplace — is a complete consumer direct capability. Combined with its current neighborhood value store, consumer direct would enable management to provide the complete shopping experience, real and virtual. I would guess that it is coming soon.

I can't imagine a Dorothy Lane manager ever asking, *"What a great idea, who else is doing it?"* Nor can I imagine them saying *"We can't do that; we are too big (or too small)."*

In fact, a quote from the founder of Dorothy Lane, which I found on their Web site, says it all; "My methods are merely common sense and a deep concern for human beings."

Here's Another Example. Scotty's Home Market in the northern suburbs of Chicago is a consumer direct (home shopping) business and then some. The company is very successful by focusing on customer relationships. In fact, half of new customers come to Scotty's through referrals; customer acquisition costs are very low as a result. Annualized retention rate is 80 percent. Remarkable!

Customers shop by fax, phone, or electronically. Overall, the average customer shops at Scotty's 24 times per year, spending $3,000. (The average orders size is $125). The company's strategy is to pursue the *profitable* customers in an area; for this reason, prices are stable and comparable to a traditional store's "fair, everyday" prices. Shoppers choose Scotty's for convenience, service, and, believe it or not, the quality of the perishables, not for deals. Fourteen percent of total volume is produce; because Scotty's has no store, produce is bought fresh every morning (like the old corner store), handled very little (because it's not exposed to shoppers), and stored in ideal temperature until it's delivered. Similarly, meats are choice grade only. The company guarantees that each item delivered is what was asked for and expected; refunds are granted and/or the item replaced immediately.

Note: the original founders of Scotty's, coming from outside the industry, depended more on innovation and common sense than capital to make this business successful. Scotty's is profitable on an order basis, doing better than $500 per square foot out of low-cost space with plenty of room to expand.

Six reasons **AGENTS** and manufacturers will work together:

1. The primary premise of the *Frictionless Marketplace* is that manufacturers and **AGENTS** anticipate and meet shoppers' needs by aligning the market attributes of the shopper with the market attributes of products. Collaboration and innovation are the only ways to achieve this alignment.

2. Money won't be a barrier (as it is today); as revenue flow matches value creation, costs will be the same for everyone.

3. The manufacturers (and shoppers) will need an **AGENT** in the future more than they need a store today. Because the **AGENT** will serve an active role in closing the gap between the *moment of desire* and the *moment of value* for each shopper, especially as technology is integrated into the lifestyle of consumers. A great opportunity for loyalty building and creating switching barriers!

4. A manufacturer will want to help the **AGENT** meet the needs of shoppers (and differentiate the shopping experience) by helping develop solutions which include its products. The opportunities for co-branding unique solutions are enormous.

5. An **AGENT** will not offer products to shoppers that are not appropriate. Initially, manufacturers may object; but, in the long run, this discrete marketing will force manufacturers to focus on their target shoppers (not waste mass money) in designing new products or re-positioning current ones. The good news is **AGENTS** will want to give manufacturers much more information about their customers' demographics and lifestyles, so manufacturers can understand the true potential of their products at each local market.

6. By working together, both will do a better job building loyalty. If an **AGENT** can show a shopper is loyal (and the shopper will benefit from being loyal because the relationship with the **AGENT** will make it easy to satisfy desires and needs), the manufacturer can choose to give her or him a special loyalty price through that **AGENT** only. Of course this loyalty option would be available to all **AGENTS** for their unique loyal shoppers.

THE COMPELLING REASON TO CHANGE - Retailer's View[38]

	TRADITIONAL STORE		AGENTRY ACTUAL STORE		AGENTRY VIRTUAL STORE		AGENTRY TOTAL		DIFFERENCE TRADITIONAL VS AGENTRY	
Sales	$300,000	100.00%	$150,000	50.00%	$150,000	50.00%	$300,000	100.00%	–	
Square Footage	40,000		10,000	25.00%	2,000	5.00%	12,000	30.00%	(28,000)	(70.00%)
Sq. Ft. Quality		100.00%		125.00%		50.00%		50.00%		
Inv. Wks. Supply	3.00		1.50		0.10					
Inv. Carry Rate		15.00%		15.00%		15.00%		15.00%		
Gross Margin	$79,500	26.50%	$45,000	30.00%	$15,000	10.00%	$60,000	20.00%	($19,500)	(24.53%)
Labor/Benefits	(42,600)	14.20%	(30,000)	20.00%	(6,000)	4.00%	(36,000)	12.00%	6,600	15.49%
Occupancy	(17,100)	5.70%	(5,344)	3.56%	(428)	0.29%	(5,771)	1.92%	11,328	66.25%
Supplies	(1,200)	0.40%	(1,125)	0.75%	(300)	0.20%	(1,425)	0.48%	(225)	(18.75%)
Inventory Costs	(1,908)	0.64%	(454)	0.30%	(39)	0.03%	(493)	0.16%	1,415	74.15%
Other	(8,580)	2.86%	(4,290)	2.86%	(4,290)	2.86%	(8,580)	2.86%	0	0.00%
Total Costs	($71,388)	23.80%	($41,213)	27.48%	($11,057)	7.37%	($52,270)	17.42%	$19,118	26.78%
Profit	$8,112	2.70%	$3,787	2.52%	$3,943	2.63%	$7,730	2.58%	($382)	(4.70%)
Sales/sq.ft.	$7.50		$15.00		$75.00		$25.00		$17.50	233%
Percentage Increase			100%		900%		233%			
Profit/sq.ft.	$0.20		$0.38		$1.97		$0.64		$0.44	220%
Percentage Increase			90%		88%		220%			

The Compelling Reasons to Change

Retailer's View

The model on page 141 is an attempt to demonstrate the overwhelming, positive impact on a retailer's financial performance as they transition to the **AGENTRY AGENDA**™. For illustrative purposes, I used industry average data in the model, and of course assumptions about the sales split between the actual and virtual stores sales. *(I recognize that each retailer's actual data is different, and in fact, will be very different store to store in AGENTRY. Therefore, I will make the Microsoft® Excel model available to you to use with your own data and your own assumptions. Just go to* AgentryAgenda.com *and send the comment* "Compelling Reason to Change Model", *and I will E-mail the model to you. I would also like any thoughts you may have after you use the model. Have a good time!)*

In summary, **AGENTRY** really represents a differentiated return on investment. Because the whole organization is leveraged around the shopping experience, labor becomes an above-the-line asset rather than a below-the-line liability. Gross margins go down, labor costs go down, occupancy costs go down, and even absolute profits go down initially. Yet, the returns on financial assets, space; and the return on marketing assets, loyal shoppers; go way up. And neither of these returns is limited by the four walls of today. There is bad news for retailers that can't divest or re-deploy excess space (non-differentiating space of $11,329 in the example): profits go from $7,730 per week to ($3,598), or from $.64 per square foot profit to ($.30) per square foot loss, on required space.

THE COMPELLING REASON TO CHANGE – Manufacturer's View

	Traditional Store	Pickup Point
Retail Price	$100	$100
Agent	(26.50)	(10)
Barrier Buster	N/A	(12)
Manufacturer	$73.50	$78

Sales Force .... (5%)

Trade Promotions .... (13%)

Redundant Inventory .... (?%)

Data Acquisition .... (?%)

The Manufacturer's View

For manufacturers, the numbers are just as good. They get a larger percentage of the sales dollar spent in the virtual store(s). At the same time, price pressures may not be as extreme as they are today, since the **AGENT** puts products in the store for "value" not as loss leaders. Remember, manufacturers will set prices virtually. These will be "benchmark prices" on which the **AGENT** bases his real store prices. In addition to the increased residual money received from the *Barrier Buster* ($78 of $100), manufacturers will achieve other benefits, including more efficient advertising, a more productive sales force, reduced operating costs (since they'll ship to only one site in a market), and better information with which to predict/replenish demand. Again, marketing will drive logistics efficiencies. Of course, product sales will increase because of the frictionless nature of the model.

One question needs to be raised: Will certain products, currently subsidized by retailers, lose their profitability? Yes, the burden of saturation will start to fall on the manufacturer. But products used by today's retailers to put more profit in their yield formulas may, in fact, increase in profitability for manufacturers since the **AGENT** takes only a standard distribution fee for the virtual sale.

Despite these compelling economics, the really important reasons to change are not financial; they are more basic than that. The **AGENTRY Model** will emerge because it is what the *shopper* wants. If a retailer or manufacturer doesn't "get on board," it will likely lose its business entirely.

Endnotes

30   It's funny that, today, stores keep getting big-
p. 114   ger and bigger so they can deliver the "one-stop shopping" concept, while shoppers find the mega-stores more and more unattractive and while the mix of what the consumer is buying is changing. Most of the research that I've seen indicates that the shopper is looking for a more immediate and intimate *moment of value* — one that can be had in both smaller stores and virtually. What a great way to grow in a flat market and, at the same time, leverage a smaller fixed infrastructure! Can we continue to assume that the shopper wants to go to bigger stores or do the retailers need to start going to the shopper?

31   The vary reason that many feel that consumer
p. 114   direct won't work in the food industry (and why it is lagging other forms of retailing in consumer direct today)- high cube and weight, low value per pound, continuously replenished to the home- is just the very reason that I think it should be leading the consumer direct movement. If we can get this working properly, what a great platform to leverage to many new growth areas.

32   The virtual side of **AGENTRY** will force the
p. 124   "natural" (i.e., market-driven) profitability of an item. The manufacturers set prices and control costs; they can make money through a volume strategy or high-quality strategy. I believe the **AGENTRY Model** conforms to FTC requirements; in fact, it may be even better than current industry practices. I believe that FedEx, ATMs, and other examples of efficient distribution have already set precedents. Also, in the fashion industry, manufacturers (Ralph Lauren and Tommy Hilfiger come to mind) have retail stores, as well as sell through department stores. Computer manufacturers sell both direct and through retailers as well. If the business model of **AGENTRY** is offered equally to everyone, it seems like fair trade to me (of course, I'm

not a lawyer!). At this stage, it's important not to be dogmatic; this is clearly a sensitive subject, with $25 billion dollars at stake!

33   In 1993, an *Andersen Consulting* study con-
p. 125   ducted for NAWGA showed that wholesalers were more efficient than self-distributing retailers. Is this surprising? After all, logistics is (or was) a core competency of wholesalers. This finding supports the *Barrier Buster* concept; the logistics productivity gains of **AGENTRY Marketing** are overwhelming and — more importantly — achievable.

Today's economics, from cost of trade promotions to the efficiencies of Internet commerce, will drive the success of the *Barrier Buster*. ECR tried to realize incremental improvements to the mass marketing model; the *Barrier Buster* would be *truly* efficient and would make the complete industry demand-and-supply chain efficient as well.

34   While outsourcing is a good way for a re-
p. 130   tailer or manufacturer to 1) improve the productivity of the distribution function and 2) focus on core competencies and issues of strategic importance, it does nothing to take redundant distribution out of the total supply chain.

35   Market level logistics is another good idea
p. 130   because it reduces redundancy within a market: Why should manufacturers, retailers, and distributors all have "same as" fleets, delivery schedules, and warehouses within one area? Does anyone have a competitive advantage because its trucks or warehouses are bigger? Not one shopper ever interviewed — at SMART STORE™ or in all its research — cared one iota how products get to the supermarket.

Market level logistics could, in fact: 1) reduce some of the forward buying and diverting in the system because the retailer typically wouldn't pay for the product until it's received at the store (and most stores have small backrooms); 2) simplify/manage the billing between the retailer and manufacturer, even consolidating bills for all products shipped to each store; 3) bring niche products to market (those products whose appeal is too limited to justify their placement in redundant warehouses); and 4) provide information to the manufacturers, such as a summary of products shipped to each store.

In short, market level logistics — not as good as a *Barrier Buster* — would still be a vast improvement over today's saturated system.

36
p. 130
By enabling *any* product to compete, the *Barrier Buster* creates the "perfect" — i.e., *Frictionless Marketplace*. Any item that meets a customer's *moment of desire* will succeed. The only variation in cost will be volume-driven; i.e., a product shipped to a store or a pick/pack center on pallets because of its high turnover will be cheaper to ship than an item sent case-by-case. These volume differences are marketing related; if a manufacturer makes a product with a limited market appeal, it should expect to have higher, *true* distribution costs.

37
p. 136
Would a wholesaler make a good *Barrier Buster*? Only if it 1) stopped buying and re-selling nationally branded products and 2) stopped being vertically integrated (i.e. owning retail stores) around the old business model. In fact, wholesalers may be most at risk when the **AGENTRY Model** takes over for the same two reasons: 1) they'll lose the inside margins they live on; and 2) they'll lack the independence. The good news is wholesalers have many of the core competencies required of the *Barrier Buster*.

38
p. 141
Notes to the Compelling Reason to Change model: 1) Model assumes virtual orders are picked up in the store. If delivered to the home, it assumes an additional delivery charge would cover the cost. 2) Virtual store square footage is to accommodate in transit pre-picked orders. 3) Square footage quality factor relates the cost of space and build-out of the base, traditional store to the **AGENTRY** space. It is used to compute the occupancy costs. 4) In the traditional store and the actual store of **AGENTRY**, the gross margin percentages are used as in traditional gross margin computations. In the case of the virtual store, the gross margin represents an estimate of the activity based costing fee that the retailer would get from the manufacturer. In the **AGENTRY Model** it would **not** be a percentage.

5. WHAT'S GOING TO HAPPEN NEXT?

As the Irishman said when asked the directions from Belfast to Dublin, *"I wouldn't start from here."*

A *Frictionless Marketplace* in the Making

For years I've been going to London, studying the marketplace and trying to understand why English food retailers are so much more profitable than U.S. retailers, especially given an intense competition among five large companies. I believe the answer is a more strategic approach to business and to customer relationships. For example, U.S. retailers implemented POS primarily to increase price control and productivity; the English used the technology to gather data they could use to run their businesses better, first with improved logistics, then with improved marketing.

Doesn't This Apply to ECR?. . ."The top management information that the new revolution is beginning to provide will make information about the outside even more important and even more urgent. All of the new concepts, from economic-chain accounting, activity-based accounting, through EVA and the executive scorecard, still provide inside information only. So, of course, does the existing MIS system. It can be argued the computer and the data flow it made possible, including the new information concepts, actually have done more harm than good to business management. They have aggravated what all along has been management's degenerative tendency, especially in the big corporations: to focus *inward* on costs and efforts, rather than outward on opportunities, changes, and threats. This threat is becoming increasingly dangerous considering the globalization of economies and industries, the rapid change in markets and in consumer behavior, the crisscrossing of technologies across traditional industry lines, and the increasing instability of currencies. The more inside information top management gets, the more it will need to balance it with outside information — and that does not exist as yet."

PETER DRUCKER, *Forbes ASAP,* AUGUST 1998

An explanation of U.K. retailers' long operating margins is twofold. First, their stores are expensive — one store might cost $50 million. They need long operating margins to cover the overhead (return on invested capital). Second, they have strong private label programs. This emphasis on self-branding and taking risks, aided in the beginning by the limits put on advertising by the government controlled media, has given the English retailers more control over the complete supply chain.

Only five years ago, I told the management of two U.K. retailers that the one spot in the world I would pick to start a *consumer direct* channel would be London, because all its economics were right:

- Urban demographics and diverse lifestyles favor more service-oriented value propositions.

- Store sites are expensive and restricted to boot, as the English say.

- Store hours were restricted at the time (not open on Sundays and limited after 6 p.m.).

- The strength of private label would encourage manufacturers to go around retailers.

At first, the retailers said they didn't want to give up the traffic in the stores. When I countered, "Wonder if someone does it [i.e., *consumer direct*] to you? — their response was a swift and simple acknowledgment of the danger of that possibility.

Now, look what London retailers are up to!

- Tesco is an Internet Service Provider.

- Tesco, Sainsbury, and Waitrose offer *consumer direct*.

- Tesco and Sainbury have small stores in the city which focus on fresh foods, home meal replacement solutions, and other AGENTRY-like amenities. In fact, Sainsbury just opened its *smallest* store — only 3,000 square feet — in decades for the expressed purpose of bringing convenience to the local community.

- Sainsbury announced its intent to help Britain's traditional village shop by agreeing to sell its own-label goods outside its own superstores.

- Tesco is starting to sell toys and apparel direct to their loyal shoppers in a joint venture to expand sales.

- Store hours have been expanded to include Sundays and 24 hours per day and even Christmas in some areas.

- Retailers are starting to share sales and inventory data with the manufacturers.

- They're all tying their loyalty cards to value-added services, such as banking and utilities.

- They're sharing logistics as mentioned before.

Go to London today and see the AGENTRY Agenda™ unfold.

Get Over It!

The transition to the *Frictionless Marketplace* could be easy if we can get past the "push back" from advocates of today's distribution model. In this last chapter, I present a few ideas for discussion; how the **AGENTRY Model** will come about *in actuality* remains to be seen. *My objective is not to define the next* *steps, but just to make the case for change.* With that in mind, here's one way the transition might happen:

- ECR leadership, supported by the industry associations, defines the **AGENTRY Model** in detail: *How will it work practically? What are the implementation steps?* Maybe ECR will have a new name: *Effective Customer Response.* A distributor and information services provider steps up to support/enable the *Barrier Buster.*

- Manufacturers start offering retailers two ways to do business: the current way or the frictionless way. Behind the offering is an analysis of value: *Could we exist in the* Frictionless Marketplace? *What are the market attributes of our products? Can our products survive without trade dollars? How can we create moments of desire? How do we organize around the needs of the* **AGENTS** *we serve? How do we manage real-time marketing?*

- Retailers begin to think of themselves as **AGENTS** for their customers, rather than distributors for manufacturers by asking: *How loyal are our shoppers? Do we create value? How good is our shopping experience? How can we do a better job capturing the moment of desire and fulfilling the moment of value? How do we organize around the local store and its shopping experience? How do we measure market performance store by store? How do we make money today? Can we make money without trade dollars?* And they need to start building the virtual shopping experience in earnest; the first one giving the shopper control will create a real switching barrier.

In response to the "push back" the **AGENTRY Model** is likely to generate, I have these arguments:

1. The simple fact is the *Barrier Buster* can drive down logistics costs for everyone. So, unless it has more than 50 percent of the market, the "big guy" could be very disadvantaged when the rest of the market signs on with the *Barrier Buster*. Also, the "big guy" wouldn't have marketing flexibility anywhere near equal to that of a *Barrier Buster*-aided **AGENT**.

2. Manufacturers don't like a retailer that uses scale against them. Hence, their fear of globalization and consolidation, which lead to more price or support cost pressures and less direct access to shoppers. The *Barrier Buster* gives the manufacturer the ultimate scale and, at the same time, returns to them control in reaching the marketplace. Best of all, it frees them from the need to spend "empty" trade dollars to bring products to market.

3. The virtual marketplace is redefining the scale advan-

tage. We already know the right virtual offering — even within the constraints of today's mass marketing model — can be as cheap (or cheaper) than any product in a profitable land-based store over time. As stated before, virtual commerce drives all prices down to the lowest common denominator.

4.   But the biggest kicker of all will be the marketing productivity made possible by the **AGENTRY Model**. While the most obvious disadvantage to companies not accepting the **AGENTRY Model** is an erosion of their leverage advantage, other implications follow suit; for example, today's organization structures and performance measurements will not enable productivity in the *Frictionless Marketplace*. Mass marketing assets — such as warehouses, truck fleets, forward buying systems, big stores, and hierarchical organizations — will suddenly lose their value and become a drain on profitability. Non-players will lack the real-time, marketing-sensitive information provided by *Barrier Busters*. Decision making will continue to be slow and cumbersome, while the rest of the market figures out how to change frequently and effortlessly.

> The first thing a retailer must do . . .define a consumer direct strategy.

Start Small; Think Big

The first thing a retailer must do (I know, I promised not to be prescriptive, but this is the single exception): **define a consumer direct strategy**. Note, I did not say "implement technology;" consumer direct is first and foremost about relationships. A Web site, while necessary in some form, should follow the consumer direct strategy, not the other way around. The number one question to address is how will I build the "shopping experience continuum" that is appropriate for my targeted shoppers?

START SMALL, THINK BIG

At the same time, a retailer must become a local market organization (LMO).

At the same time, a retailer must become a local market organization (LMO). If **AGENTRY** implies building unique relationships with shoppers and — even more importantly — anticipating their needs, then employees in the stores will be the most important people in the company. Employees will have an increasing impact on a store's performance and differentiation. This statement has significant implications for most retailers.

Today's senior management grew up in a system of central buying and standardized stores; to solve the problems of saturation, industry executives try putting cross-functional teams on top of still-rigid and top-heavy organizations. The bigger the company, the worse it gets.

A case in point: how retailers and manufacturers use information. Most suck the data out of the store and send it to headquarters, where analysts pore over it, looking for clues to the secret of competitive advantage. But the secret is not in the products; it's in the customer's satisfaction with the shopping experience. Sure, it makes sense to localize assortments, even down to the individual-shopper level; but that's not all there is to a "shopping experience."

Independents (and a few good, big retailers) know better. Wegmans is decentralized in its organization, at least as it applies to the fresh part of the store, as are Hy-Vee and Carrefour. In the **AGENTRY Model**, big — in and of itself — is not a good thing. What's important to the shopper? Probably the cashier (especially if she smiles), the informative produce manager, or the butcher; for sure "their store".

Who's running the business like this today? In Feargal Quinn's stores (Superquinn) in Ireland, I saw an example of what I'm talking about here: a young man, whose job was squeezing fresh orange juice, found out shoppers would prefer to see a "day" rather than a "date" stamped on the lid of the juice. He suggested the change; it was approved, and he was asked to implement the new practice in all 16 stores. (How long would it take the typical chain of 100 stores to implement a similar change with its market specialists and ROI analysts?) This employee listens to the store's customers and applies what he learns to improve the shopping experience. He has had an impact on shopper satisfaction and on his own job satisfaction.

> He has had an impact on shopper satisfaction and on his own job satisfaction.

From the Bottom, Up

At SMART STORE™, reseach suggested that the retailer start the reorganization effort at the local market level by thinking of each store as a *"chain of one"* — Dorothy Lane is a good model. Suddenly, the importance of employees becomes apparent: they are in the store, interacting with shoppers. They are the eyes and ears of management. And, in turn, they represent the **AGENT** (retailer) in the minds of the company's customers. It's critically important that store employees be relevant, because they *are* relevant; they need to have authority to improve the shopping experience. They are the single, best source of information about shoppers' needs and frustrations; such information will never come out of POS systems. Remember: franchise stores outperform corporate stores.

> It's critically important that store employees be relevant, because they are relevant . . .

THE STORE EMPLOYEE IS THE EYES & EARS OF MANAGEMENT

CORPORATE MANAGEMENT

STORE MANAGEMENT

STORE EMPLOYEE

HI MRS. SMITH!

Overall, the retailer's organization would be built on a structure of "market modules" in which a limited number of stores — say, 10 — are grouped because of a common profile, perhaps demographics or geography or (in most cases) both. Why get any bigger than this? Each module would be led by people who are responsible for making each store relevant to its shoppers and employees. In this "marketing" organization, stores are positioned strategically and profitably, given the needs of local consumers and the presence of local competition. Decision makers are measured on store market performance and long-time shopper loyalty. This model duplicates the organizations of innovative, independent retailers, such as Ukrop's, D&W Food Centers, and Superquinn. Why get any bigger? These independents are big enough to have marketing skills and marketing scale, but small enough to address each shopper's needs.

Decision makers are measured on store market performance and long-time shopper loyalty.

MARKET MODULE

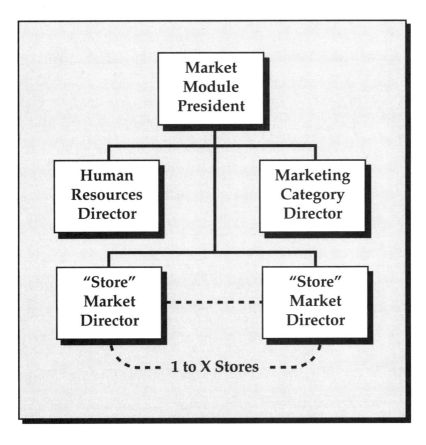

The market Performance of an Independent

This "chain of one" structure makes it easy to customize the market offerings and the shopping experience in each store.

Economic Value Added will be measured store-by-store and even shopper-by-shopper because each AGENT will "differentiate differently".

This *"chain of one"* structure makes it easy to customize the market offerings and the shopping experience in each store. The market module team decides the role of each category and each service as a means to increase each store's performance and each shopper's satisfaction. These small modules allow change to be rolled out in parallel and, at the same time, adjusted to the needs of the marketplace. Higher up the organization, a "Chief Demand Officer" is responsible for corporate-level activities: new business opportunities, new solution ideas, merchandising innovations, new channel development, and strategic planning. (See chart on page 161)

Similarly, manufacturers should start running their businesses *customer by customer* (i.e., **AGENT**/retailer by **AGENT**/retailer), *not at the chain level but at the store level.* Two common-sense facts make this important: 1) with today's consolidation and globalization, fewer and fewer retailers make up a larger and larger percentage of each manufacturer's business; and 2) each retailer will progress toward **AGENTRY** at its own pace; in the interim, manufacturers will need to be flexible in how they structure relationships. Also, once **AGENTRY** is widespread, Economic Value Added will be measured store-by-store and even shopper-by-shopper because each **AGENT** will "differentiate differently". While brands will continue to be important in the future, the operating and financial performance of a manufacturer will be driven by its ability to maximize its potential with each **AGENT**/retailer. One practical implication is that money will be spent in accordance to each **AGENT'S** needs and marketing strategies.

Linking the **AGENT** to the manufacturer are "Marketing Category Managers" whose objective is to create a shopper-sensitive range of assortments — at SMART STORE™ ,they were called "Strategic Marketing Assortments" or SMAs — which fulfill the marketing strategies defined by the market modules for each store. This is important: the SMAs' strategies are defined by the marketing needs of the stores, not by the category managers or manufacturers. Remember: a category is not a stand-alone business unit; it's part of a shopping experience.

Remember: a category is not a stand-alone business unit; it's part of a shopping experience.

SAME RETAILER, DIFFERENT STORES

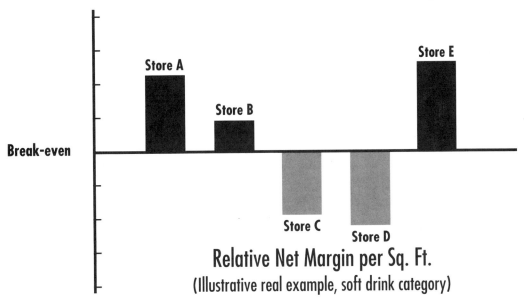

Relative Net Margin per Sq. Ft.
(Illustrative real example, soft drink category)

Most chains would have five or six SMAs for each category. An obvious example is pet foods. The pet food section in an urban area would differ from one in a rural area. Even the less obvious categories have store to store variations. While "Marketing Category Managers" support the needs of each actual store, the market module team is in control. Manufacturers work with the Marketing Category Managers to match their product attributes with the SMAs and to devise store-by-store strategies for their products.

The core competency that matters — to both **AGENTS** and manufacturers — is understanding the customers, not dis-

Stretegic Marketing Assortment Process

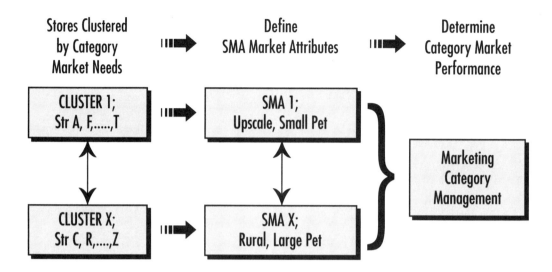

Stores Clustered by Category Market Needs	Define SMA Market Attributes	Determine Category Market Performance
CLUSTER 1; Str A, F,.....,T	SMA 1; Upscale, Small Pet	
CLUSTER X; Str C, R,....,Z	SMA X; Rural, Large Pet	Marketing Category Management

tributing product. In other words, the manufacturer needs to understand SMA concepts and other components of the **AGENT'S** organization so it can help the **AGENT** put the right products in the actual stores — those products that create value, as perceived by shoppers. If the **AGENT** is going to take risks by offering items (or not offering items) to customers, then the trust between manufacturer and **AGENT** needs to be high. In a mass market store, a retailer can promote anything; in an **AGENTRY** store, the shopping experience is too important for the **AGENT** to risk alienating customers.

A key concept in this new organization is interpretive change.

A key concept in this new organization is *interpretive change*.[39] The **AGENT'S** organization has to treat each store differently; the question of whether to introduce a new solution, service offering, and/or product has to be discrete; that is, each local store should decide what makes sense for its own shoppers. The local store management will *interpret* recommendations or suggestions, and create unique ideas for their own store that can be fed back up through the module and organization to be shared with similar stores in the chain. Likewise, the manufacturer will *interpret* the role of a product in any given market. Using our pet food example, demand for pet food in a neighborhood of urban, high-rise apartment buildings would likely differ from demand in a rural or suburban neighborhood where houses are separated by relatively large tracks of land. But the urban, high rise demand can be used in planning a new urban, high rise store, or benchmarking the categories performance

CROSS FUNCTIONAL RETAILER

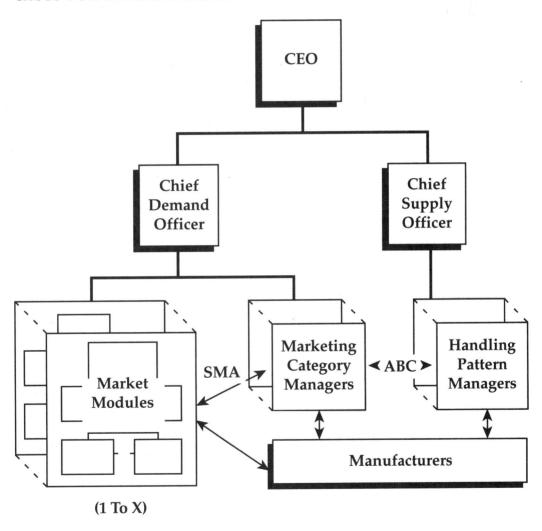

against other like urban, high rise stores. As the industry moves to virtual selling, this need for interpretive change at store level will become even more important because the real store will only have room for products of value to the shoppers in that store.

THE DEMAND SIDE PROCESS

– – – – AGENT/Manufacturer Alliance Opportunity

An LMO (Local Market Organization) supports the demand/supply concept. The two processes are connected, complementary, logical, and measured appropriately.

Since the supply side's objective is to minimize the delivered cost to the store shelf or even to the shopper's home, an **AGENT** must know its handling patterns and their costs. A typical supermarket has 20-25 handling patterns *distinct enough* to measure; for example, the cost of receiving and shipping by pallet to a store versus receiving by pallet and shipping by case. Retailers need to measure these handling patterns *as they are today* so they can evaluate the option of a *Barrier Buster* in the future. The Chief Supply Officer in the LMO may not have any logistics assets of his own (other than the measurement of performance of the handling patterns); because a *Barrier Buster*'s value will be obvious when measured against current internal performance.

THE SUPPLY SIDE PROCESS

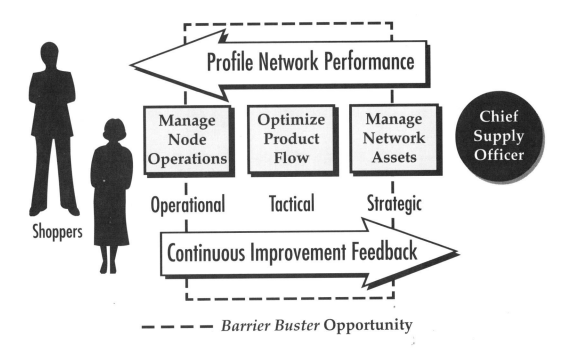

Start Measuring the Right Things

In the *Frictionless Marketplace*, the goal is not cost cutting; the goal is increasing *yield* through value creation. *Yield* — measured store by store (actual and virtual) and shopper by shopper — depends on the **AGENT'S** mix of products, services, ambiance, virtual interface, and employees. Differentiation comes from the shopping experience, from providing better solutions, information, and other value-added variables.

AND THE SIZE OF THE HOOD ORNAMENT IS...

HOW BIG IS THE ENGINE?

STORE

START MEASURING THE RIGHT THINGS

> **Yield management means balancing financial performance with market performance of the aggregate "store,"...**

Yield management means balancing financial performance with market performance of the aggregate "store," made up of the sum of its parts, virtual and real store parts, and category and service parts. (this is why benchmarking is so out-of-touch with local market realities). The challenge at "store" level is to: 1) profile the store's (and the shoppers') potential (actual and virtual shopping); 2) analyze the store's competition; 3) decide what groups of products and services to put in the store; and 4) define expectations for their role/volume in the store's overall market performance. These decisions and definitions are not "standard"; rather, they are specific to the shoppers and competitors in the area. Some chains will emphasize return on square feet (financial productivity), while others will measure return on loyal shoppers (marketing productivity); the best will keep track of both. For sure they will differ, store by store.

Markets change in a hurry (and that change is accelerated by saturation). That's why profiling is so important. Without a profile of the store's market *potential* (and the ability to report against it), the **AGENT** has no way to improve the store's performance or find out when it is going south. Profiling starts with an analysis of the store's market conditions, consumers, and competitors. Then, shoppers are profiled according to types of households, number of target households, etc. The **AGENT** needs feedback here because *potential* should not be based on last year's sales, or on the ranking of the store in the chain, or on prior profits, or even on loyal shoppers. Rather, *potential* should mean: *How many of the store's shopper are loyal? How many of the loyal shoppers are target shoppers and vice versa? How effective are our marketing programs?* Similarly, *potential* is not defined as "staying ahead of competitors"; rather, it means, "staying ahead of the shoppers."

At the chain level, *yield management* means maximizing the potential of each market module (by managing each store to its potential) and optimizing the shopper life cycle. (See the discussion of shopper loyalty on page 54). Real wealth comes from long-term customer loyalty, and long-term loyalty comes from anticipating and satisfying shoppers' needs.

I have always wanted to do a research project comparing the market performance and profitability of a good independent store with that of a store in a large chain, fully costed. I would bet that, even without all the distribution "advantage," the independents are much more effective in their marketplace and much more profitable store by store. They understand yield as it relates to the shopping experience.

In my experience most manufacturers think about category management at the chain level, thinking of the chain as one big store; and therefore managing to average. This is my challenge to manufacturers: *Select five stores from your favorite retailer and look at the performance of your category by return on square footage (the financial measure) and return on loyal shoppers (the marketing measure).*

> ...potential is not defined as "staying ahead of competitors"; rather, it means, "staying ahead of the shoppers."

> ...most manufacturers think about category management at the chain level...

The difference from store to store — a marketing productivity gap — is an opportunity available today (see chart on page 159).

Measurements for manufacturers will change, too — from a brand focus to a store orientation and even an individual shopper focus. Traditional market-share measurements won't be relevant anymore. The new question, of course, will be: *What is the potential for a brand among target shoppers served by a specific* **AGENT**? In other words, every product will not sell in every **AGENT'S** customer set. Yet, the power of the manufacturer to market brands directly to consumers will actually increase in the **AGENTRY Model**. Because the manufacturer will set the price in the virtual store, and they will get feedback from the **AGENT** about sales, store by store, customer segment by customer segment. They will also create moments of desire (instantly captured with technology) through advertising and promotions (the way manufacturers created a huge demand by exploiting the new technology of television in the Development phase).

...the power of the manufacturer to market brands directly to consumers will actually increase in the AGENTRY Model.

As the industry transforms from a logistics model to a marketing model, the **AGENT** will collect information about, and measure the performance of, each store. The **AGENT** will want to share this information with manufacturers to get their help and support. The technology to capture the measurements of a *Frictionless Marketplace* — everything from on-time delivery and out-of-stocks to the success of solutions and the customer's delight with the shopping experience — exists today. All that's needed is the right attitude.

This will put extreme pressures on manufacturers' organizations as they shift from a brand focus to a customer, local market focus; especially when the customers are going global. While brands will be very important in the *Frictionless Marketplace*, so will individual stores and shoppers. With timely feedback from the *Barrier Buster*, manufacturers will have the opportunity to do "real-time marketing," watching how sales (for sure virtually and probably by actual store) result from advertising and other stimulants and to make real-time adjustments accordingly. Each shopper will be different; each **AGENT** will be different; and each "store" will become different. Manufacturers will put people back in the field (at least in trend setting markets), working with the **AGENTS** in trying to achieve optimal market performance. The sharing of knowledge between markets and from **AGENT** to **AGENT** will be important because the key information will not be the "cold" market share data used today. Rather, it will be shoppers' attitudes and satisfaction. Unfortunately, in many ways, ECR moved organizations in the opposite direction.

Unfortunately, in many ways, ECR moved organizations in the opposite direction.

A New Worldview

As I hope this book makes clear, I see dramatic changes coming for this industry. What can we expect in terms of performance improvements? Here are a few ideas I have; I'm sure anyone still with me at this point will think of many more. These observations are not precise or scientific; in most cases, I didn't even try to put an economic value on the new ways we'll be conducting business. The purpose of this book has been — from the beginning — to explore new ideas. I look forward to hearing your reactions (use **AgentryAgenda.com**) and seeing what really develops!

Shopper Productivity

1. Shoppers have one source for products, their **AGENT**. There's no need to shop store to store for national brands since they are available virtually at one, consistent price. The **AGENT** will be selected according to how well it matches the shopper's value proposition.

2. Virtual shopping makes the replenishment of core items "one click" or "one scan" away.

3. The small, value-driven, neighborhood **AGENTRY Model** stores are close to the shopper's home. Their local market focus makes it easy for the shopper to shop. Yet, the shopper has easy, virtual access to any item which any manufacturer puts into the marketplace — potentially 100,000-200,000 items — not available in one store today. *ECR objective of efficient assortment is achieved.*

4. Shoppers need an **AGENT** so they can order through WebTV, or personal computers (or their equivalent), and/or light pens (and similar technologies, integrated into lifestyles) in the home. The **AGENT** captures the shopper's *moments of desire* as they're created. Shopping is a 7-days-a-week, 24-hours-a-day process — almost unconscious, really.

5. Because of better differentiation among **AGENTS'** stores, shopping takes less time; also, the shopper makes fewer errors since information (about products, services, etc.) is plentiful. So are knowledgable employees.

. . .ECR objective of efficient assortment is achieved.

6. In the quest for creating a loyal shopper, the **AGENT** sorts out products inappropriate for the shopper, thereby eliminating a lot of the clutter which exhausts shoppers today.

7. The opportunity for the manufacturer and **AGENT** to work together on real loyalty (to stores and products) ensures loyal shoppers get the best price. Coupled with the virtual prices on national brands, this minimizes the use of price to encourage switching from one brand to another.

8. The shopper does not need to handle and transport many items (core and other) to the home.

9. Shopping in the actual store becomes fun again. And the shopper has much more time to do other things.

AGENT Productivity

1. The entire organization is focused on shoppers and building their loyalty. The *Barrier Buster* handles the supply side. Accounting is simple since accounts payables are reduced to once-a-week statements. **AGENTS** become marketers, whose No. 1 asset is a loyal customer base. Over time, this loyalty drives the market value of the business.

2. The **AGENT** adapts its actual stores to meet the needs of the local neighborhood and its virtual stores to meet the needs of the individual household. Better than managing to average (where every store is treated the same), this focus is the basis for building loyalty. Yet, the **AGENT** can offer many more items than is possible today. This possibility is very important for meeting special needs, such as medical diets or functional foods.

3. The marketing information an **AGENT** gets is complete, since it includes all the purchases of the shopper, actual and virtual. (There's no reason for the shopper to "shop

around" for national brands since prices are the same everywhere. In fact, the shopper will want to use one **AGENT** because "switching" would be a hassle. Also, the loyal shopper is rewarded by the **AGENT** and manufacturer.)

4. Assuming the loyal shopper is an efficient shopper (see page 60), the store uses shopper feedback to improve its offerings. New customers cost less to acquire (because of referrals).

5. Advertising takes a different turn, as **AGENTS** look for customers who fit each store's profile. Money is spent to generate referrals and for targeting.

6. Although the stores are smaller and more focused, a large trading area is possible because of synergy with the virtual "store." Stores encourage "communities of interest" (an Internet concept). For example, a store might target "loft dwellers" (i.e., young, urban professionals with shared needs) even if they don't all live in the same neighborhood.

7. The actual store is much different, focused on the shopping experience and value creation. It's a fun place to work. Employees are involved in merchandising, suggesting innovation, encouraging shopper loyalty, moving tasks from below the value line (such as stocking shelves) to activities above the line (such service selling). Employee turnover falls dramatically.

8. Most important, the **AGENT** realizes a much greater return on high-cost financial assets. (Remember, the trade dollars and resulting gross margins we enjoy today will erode rapidly as virtual shopping takes hold.) In the **AGEN-TRY Model**, the key financial measurement is differentiated return on space, not gross margin or allowance dol-

lars. And because the **AGENT** can expand its offerings far beyond the limits of today's store, it can leverage much larger sales and loyalty with much less space.

Manufacturer Productivity

1. A big gain comes from the reduction or redeployment of trade dollars/costs — an estimated total $33 billion today. Even more important than the dollars are the time and effort which will be saved in this area. (This is a key economic force behind the **AGENTRY AGENDA**™).

2. Every shopper has access (virtual) to every product the manufacturer wants to risk by putting it in the marketplace at an appropriate price. Promotions (directed to shoppers through the Internet) are adjusted based on real-time marketing information. *Two more ECR objectives (efficient new item introductions and efficient promotions) are achieved.*

3. The manufacturer also redirects much of its organization to marketing, which approaches "real-time". Solution teams work with **AGENTS** to match products' market attributes to the shoppers' attributes, thereby helping the **AGENT** create more value.

4. The manufacturer creates desire for its products in many ways. The shoppers desire is automatically captured through interactive TV, the Internet, or light pens; assisted by the **AGENT**, which improves the conversion rate substantially. (That sure beats coupons.)

5. Advertising is much more effective, as the manufacturer targets the shoppers it wants. This is done through the Internet or direct mail or in conjunction with the **AGENT** through its actual or virtual stores. Obviously, the more

Two more ECR objectives (efficient new item introductions and efficient promotions) are achieved.

171

targeted the advertising, the better it wins the business of the shopper. (Remember, the **AGENT** will want the help of the manufacturer in winning the loyalty of the shoppers; there will be no false economics.)

6. Through the **AGENT**, the manufacturer has the chance to spend marketing dollars rewarding loyal shoppers (which also helps the **AGENT** build loyalty with the shopper). Loyalty pricing may be much less expensive then the current trade dollars or "switching" dollars. Overall, marketing is much more effective.

7. The **AGENTRY Model** permits niche products to reach the intended customers (these products do not always get through today's volume model). Almost by definition, most new products are focused on smaller and smaller segments of the population, and **AGENTS** will become more important as new developments in "functional foods" and other specialty items require focused marketing and flexible logistics to succeed.

8. **AGENTS** help the manufacturer with product design, based on the reactions of shoppers in the stores. They may even look for ways to co-brand with the manufacturers, while the manufacturers (as experts in the use of their products) are connected (through store kiosks or Web site links) to shoppers with questions.

9. Marketing data is better than ever, approaching "real-time." (Manufacturers help **AGENTS** carry the right items in their stores.) Manufacturers know product movement by actual store, virtual store, and shopper segment. Promotion effectiveness at store level is easily tracked because the dollars are paid based on point-of-sale activity. In addition, with the **AGENT** wanting to

capture the *moment of desire*, the manufacturer gets much better data about the effectiveness of its promotions by shopper segment and media.

10. An improvement in the economics of logistics is a by-product of the improvements in marketing productivity. For example, the industry might have one-fourth the SKU points in twice as many actual stores (compared to today, see page 128).

11. Each product will compete on its own market merit; there will be no subsidizing of one product by another.

Barrier Buster Productivity

1. Only one logistics system supports the network. The six or so warehouses operated by the retailers and wholesalers in any given market today, and all the manufacturers' warehouses, are combined into one regional distribution system. Overall, inventory is reduced four-fold (or more). There's no deal-driven inventory in the system because the **AGENTRY Model** takes away those incentives. Also, inventory in each store is localized and contributing to a *moment of value*. Instead of carrying 110 laundry items, the store carries ten for convenience, while the others are available virtually if the manufacturer wants to support them in the market.

2. The **AGENTRY Model** provides the opportunity to manage logistics as one system with complete inventory visibility, from the store to the manufacturer. Out-of-stocks should no longer be a problem in stores. This is also very important as we move to localized, *moment of value* merchandising. One system can get niche products to the store more effectively, while difficult-to-manage areas (like frozen foods and health and beauty products) get better ser-

vice, possibly once-per-day deliveries because of the order density created by a unified system.

3. The **AGENTRY Model** puts the management of the logistics system under one professional group dedicated to the improvement of its performance. Fees are activity-based and consistent. **AGENTS** can devote all their attention to winning the loyalty of their shoppers; manufacturers have a much easier process of demand planning since everything goes through one system. It's much easier for the manufacturer's operations group to adjust to market changes.

ECR objective of effieient replentishment is achieved.

4. The transportation system is more efficient. Inbound transportation goes to only one point in each market (versus the five to six points typical in large markets today). More frequent shipments by manufactures enables quicker response to market changes. Outbound logistics is also more efficient because of the density of delivery within a market. *ECR objective of effieient replentishment is achieved.*

5. Since payment for product occurs as it enters the actual store or when the shopper buys it virtually, accounting becomes much simpler; in fact, it resembles a transfer system, effectively using a standard price for nationally branded products. The problems of accounts payable and receivable go away. Again, this lets both **AGENT** and manufacturer redeploy their efforts towards winning shopper loyalty through outstanding shopping experiences and products.

6. Probably the most important logistics productivity gain comes from the *Barrier Buster* enabling consumer direct to be efficient and effective. Everyone wants this! When manufacturers can connect directly to the shopper through an **AGENT**, consumer direct will be economically viable. Prices for most products will likely fall, as will the cost of

shopping to the shopper. The ability to capture the *moment of desire* through an **AGENT** will improve the productivity of product flow in anticipating and fulfilling the demand created.

7. The infrastructure established by the *Barrier Buster* for high weight and cube, but low value, food items delivered by the **AGENT** to the consumer will be easily leveraged to other products and services, again increasing the productivity of the investment.

8. There will be one standard system, connecting **AGENTS**, manufacturers, and *Barrier Busters*, with a flow of product, funds, and information. This not only provides consistent data so all players make decisions from the same "page," it also saves substantial connect time that can better be used for marketing purposes.

INDUSTRY PRODUCTIVITY BY PHASE

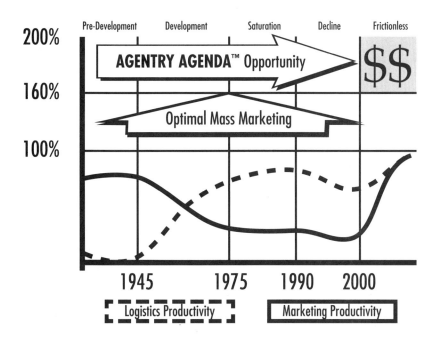

175

Productivity over the Phase (Chart page 175)

The fundamental message of SMART STORE™ has been to maximize demand side processes (marketing) and supply side processes (logistics). In the preface I mention the objectives of these two processes; in ten years, not one person has ever disagreed with their importance. Yet, we are a long way from achieving 100 percent performance in these two processes. Even more distressing, the industry's performance will only get worse unless we change our basic business model.

The **AGENTRY AGENDA**™ is one way the industry can approach optimal performance for a simple reason: this model aligns organizations, measurements, and processes, while *matching revenues and risks with the creation of value as defined by the consumer.* While the demand side processes and supply side processes are interdependent, the demand side drives the supply side. Failure to understand this will perpetuate less-than-optimal performance. This chart shows the productivity of marketing (from the consumer's perspective) and logistics over the five phases of the industry. It shows the productivity opportunity in adopting the **AGENTRY AGENDA**™.

- In the Pre-Development phase, there was no logistics as we know it today. Delivery of product was direct to each neighborhood store. Not especially efficient! Yet, the performance of marketing may have been close to its peak assuming its measurement to be "achieving each store's market potential." In fact, I estimate the marketing productivity of this phase to be 70-80 percent (not more because of the lack of national brands available to the local market and because of small store size). The customer was very satisfied with the shopping experience.

- In the Development phase, the logistics productivity of central buying and distribution became obvious; it became, in fact, the driver of the mass marketing model. I estimate a logistics productivity level of about 70-80 percent (not more because of redundancy in the marketplace). At the same time, marketing productivity declined because of the shift from the individual relationship to mass marketing with its "every store is the same" efficiency. Also, many products do not make it to market because they cannot justify (logistically) a spot in the warehouse. National advertising offsets this to some extent by generating demand for new products. The shopper becomes a consumer.

- In the Saturation phase, the productivity of both demand and supply processes takes a hit. Redundancy, forward buying, and diverting hurt the overall performance of logistics. Saturation of products and promotional messages, as well as price confusion and the introduction of alternative formats, hurt the performance of marketing. The escalation of trade dollar spending says it all. The shopping experience becomes hard work.

- In the Decline phase, saturation reaches a higher pitch. Sophisticated management techniques, such as category management, activity-based costing, and loyalty programs, are applied to the same old organizations, measurements, and business practices. Management moves further away from shoppers. Sales per square foot declines 17.2 percent from 1991 through 1997, the ECR years.

- In the Frictionless phase, both processes have the potential of reaching 100 percent performance because of industry alignment with shopper needs. The only determinant will be the ability (or inability) of an organization *"to earn the right to anticipate and deliver products and services which fulfill the needs and expectations of individual customers, whether through a virtual or actual store, because of relationships built on trust."*

A Full Cycle: The Old Becomes New, Again

The new *Frictionless Marketplace* will resurrect many of the values of the old Pre-Development phase. For example, the old neighborhood store created a community of interest; it served as a central meeting place, often bringing together neighbors in a social context valuable in and of itself. Similarly, the AGENT would create a community of interest, not just in its entertaining, customer-focused actual stores, but through the information provided via the virtual store.

The store continuum (actual and virtual) will be designed (in format and content) to match local shoppers' demographics and to compete on the shopping experience. An urban store would be different from a suburban store; a store in Texas would be different from a store in New York. In the Pre-Development phase, the owner ran the store; merchandising and service were completely decentralized (a chain of one). In the *Frictionless Marketplace*, organization structures and measurement systems will enable each store continuum to make decisions as if it were a chain of one. In fact, centralization will be a real competitive disadvantage.

In summary, the *Frictionless Marketplace* puts the shopper at the center of the industry — *again*. What could be better for the consumer products industry?

THE INDUSTRY CHANGE!

Mass Marketing	Past
Local Marketing	**Current**
AGENTRY AGENDA™	Future

Where Are You?

Endnotes

39 In a recent issue of *Harvard*
p. 160 *Business Review* (March-April 1998) Richard K. Lester, Michael J. Piore, and Kamal M. Malek describe interpretive management vis-à-vis product design. "When there is such a high degree of uncertainty, the development effort is better understood as an open-ended process rather than as a project in which a specific problem is solved. The role of [management] is not so much one of analysis or problem solving as it is of *interpreting* the new situation — listening to and talking with customers ... and discerning the new possibilities that open up through those interactions. Interpretation, no less than invention, is a highly creative process ... The interpretive manager ... embraces ambiguity and improvisation as essential to innovation." (page 89)

Conclusion

I would like to conclude this book with an anecdote.

A couple of years ago, I participated in a SMART STORE™ three-hour presentation to a group of 300 management representatives from manufacturing companies in Canada. The topic was the future of the food industry. Afterward, a panel including the CEO of a major Canadian retailer, discussed the issues presented. When asked what he thought about the possibilities of consumer direct, the CEO said, "We'll decide to move to consumer direct when we feel it makes sense for us." Another panel member, the Canadian president of a major manufacturer, aggressively replied, "We'll reach the consumer with you or around you." Hardly a frictionless relationship. And hardly what the shopper wants.

I believe that this story says it all. And it's been confirmed during confidential conversations I've had with manufacturers all over the world. This tension is symptomatic of the false economics of the mass marketing model applied to today's market conditions of saturation and no growth. Today's ECR efforts can't fix this. Consolidation and globalization will only make it worse.

The **AGENTRY AGENDA**™ *is not a possibility in the future; it's an inevitability. Like all change, it will be driven by outside forces, in this case the shopper, armed with new technology and information, as well as the power and desire to cut through the industry's false economics. And isn't that where the power should reside if we call ourselves the consumer products industry?*

Change will also be driven by economics. Manufacturers will stop spending trade dollars once they have the opportunity to invest the money (and effort) in reaching consumers directly. The threat to "go around you" comes from frustration and anger. But, in practical reality, the manufacturer will need an agent; and an agent will need the manufacturer. The shopper needs both.

I know many of you have found this book provocative if not extreme. Good! But, as I said in the preface, the inspiration for this book is you — the retailers and manufacturers I've talked to over the years at SMART STORE™, in stores, at production plants, and in corporate boardrooms. This book is my attempt to interpret your ideas.

Please, read Appendix I, The Principles of Agentry Comparison, and see if you agree. If you do, then let's use the **AGENTRY AGENDA**™ *to start a movement toward the Frictionless Phase of this industry. It will be very rewarding.*

Thank you for inspiration and your interest.

GLEN TERBEEK

Principles of AGENTRY AGENDA™ Comparison

Principle	AGENTRY	Mass
1 Match Revenues with Value Created	1. **AGENT** pays for product only when received in real store, since they assume the local market acceptance or solution risk associated with having the product in the store. No chance for inside margins. 2. **AGENT** only receives activity based distribution fee for virtual sales of national brands since the **AGENT** only provides a "capture of desire" and distribution service for the product. 3. Promotion dollars are only paid on POS sales for real store promotions, and thus real consumer performance. 4. Manufacturers assume all costs and risks for their products until received in the real store or sold virtually.	1. Slotting allowances, failure allowances, global discounts. 2. Gross margins. 3. Forward buying, diverting, inside margins. 4. Load the retailer for quarterly results.
2 Eliminate All Barriers	1. **AGENT** has equal access to all national brands in the marketplace through the *Barrier Buster*, at the same cost in the real store and at the standard distribution fee for virtual sales. 2. Manufacturers have instantaneous access to all consumers virtually through any **AGENT** because of the *Barrier Buster*. **AGENT** is rewarded equally in getting their customer any national branded item desired. 3. Size and scale will have no direct impact on national branded product costs since buying and reselling are eliminated and *Barrier Buster* enables a much lower logistics cost, standard for all **AGENTS**.	1. Big guys get the capacity, global discounts, buying power. 2. Slotting allowances, global discounts, store size limitations, logistics economic restrictions. 3. Consolidation, globalization.
3 Minimize Industry Conflicts	1. National brand prices are standard for all **AGENTS** and are available to all **AGENTS** for both real and virtual stores. 2. Allowances are paid for actual performance. 3. There is complete access to all national branded items by the shopper and there is complete access to all shoppers by the manufacturer. 4. The **AGENT** will help the manufacturer by capturing the consumer's desire that is created by the manufacturer and converting it into moment of value. 5. Funds transfers by *Barrier Buster* at standard market costs and / or fees will eliminate cost related conflicts. 6. The only "conflicts" will be matching the market attributes of products to market attributes of shoppers for real stores. 7. **AGENTS** will select manufactures as their category experts for real or virtual stores and work together to respond to the shoppers' need for answers.	1. Are you kidding? 2. Forward buying, diverting, invoice deductions. 3. Alternative formats, store size limitations, central-ized merchandising and category decisions, store pricing confusion on national branded products. 4. Slotting allowances, global discounts, trade dollars. 5. Invoice deductions, unsaleables, DSD systems. 6. Every manufacturer wants to go around the retailer. 7. Category captain fees.

Principle

AGENTRY

Mass

Principle	AGENTRY	Mass
4. Level the Playing Field	1. Availability, access, and cost will not play to the advantage of any **AGENT** or manufacturer regardless of size. 2. Competition will be reduced to innovation and creating market desire for both the shopping experience for the **AGENT** and market product qualities for national branded products and the matching of both to capture shopper loyalty. 3. "Unlevel playing fields" result for **AGENTS** which create the best shopping experience and for manufacturers which create the best products and the desire for them. 4. The *Barrier Buster* will enable innovative new **AGENTS** and new products to compete with much less capital. 5. Information will be a natural by product. All will have equal access. It is what is done with the information that will differentiate. Employee information will be a more important source, since POS doesn't tell shopper satisfaction and or reactions.	1. Enough said above. 2. Scale, market share, productivity of the logistics system. 3. Are you kidding? 4. Scale and the organizations that result stifle innovation. 5. POS data is sold, but not shared. Consumer research is big business.
5. Encourage Innonvation and its Rapid, Interpretive Rollout	1. **AGENT** organizations will become decentralized to the store level. There is little to do centrally and the competitive battle will be market by market. Manufacturers will need to execute at the **AGENT**/market level. Both will be much closer to the shopper. Rollout of innovation will happen in parallel **and** interpreted to the local market needs. 2. False distribution profits will be eliminated. Building loyalty to products and shopping experience will be the only way to compete and be successful. 3. **AGENTS** and manufacturers working locally will together create market level accepted solutions that differentiate in the attempt to win loyalty.	1. Consolidation and globalization is driven by buying power and central services savings. Decision making moves further away from the shopper. Committee meetings, consumer research, return on investment analysis and fear of change replace common sense. 2. Scale, forward buying, diverting, trade dollars, and large, "remote" organizartions. 3. Whose brand is more important?
6. Build Real Loyalty for Retailers and Brands	1. **AGENTS** and manufacturers will build loyalty programs based on the lifecycle of the shopper. 2. Loyalty programs will be based on rewarding true loyalty. The more the shopper shops or buys products, the more he or she is rewarded. 3. **AGENTS** and manufacturers will build joint loyalty programs that help each other as well as reward the shopper. 4. **AGENTS** and manufacturers will build real switching barriers through the virtual relation-ship. The concept of one click loyalty will become real. This will be enhanced in the real store through the proper local marketing and overall store ambiance.	1. A customer is a $25 transaction. Loyalty programs are another way to get deal money from the manufacturer. 2. Loyalty programs are new pricing gimmicks. 3. Marketing programs are designed for switching. 4. The average shopper has 2 to 3 loyalty cards.

AGENTRY

Principle	AGENTRY	Mass
7. Align Organizations, Measurements and Core Compentencies with Consumer Values	1. **AGENTS** are organized around local markets and individual shoppers. They will measure performance around satisfaction of loyal targeted shoppers. That will be their only opportunity for profits and long-term wealth creation. 2. Manufacturers will be organized around their **AGENT** customers. Penetration of the real stores potential (market share) as defined by the **AGENT'S** targeted shoppers will be the long term success measurement. Manufacturers will also organize their real-time marketing efforts for virtual sales around the local markets. Success will be measured on the penetration of targeted consumer segments and the conversion rate for their moment of desire strategies. 3. *Barrier Busters* will only be focused on the most efficient and effective logistics system, measured in lowest possible total cost delivered to the end consumer.	1. Retailers are organized around categories, and measured on sales increases, gross margin and deal money. 2. Manufacturers are organized around brands and mass market channels. 3. Marketing dollars destroy any hope of achieving optimal logistics efficiency.
8. Build a Platform for Growth	1. Once a shopper's relationship is built on trust, the **AGENT** is able to expand their offering to other products and services breaking out of the flat or declining market of supermarkets. This will be done with real and virtual relationships. 2. Manufacturers will have frictionless access to shoppers virtually and more influence at the local store. They will have "real-time" marketing information. Their working knowledge of the shoppers' reactions to ads and promotions and store performance will help in product improvement and new item introductions. 3. **AGENTS** and manufacturers will have easy, barrier-free access to the markets with the only barrier their ability to compete. 4. Long-term market capitalization growth will be based on loyalty. **AGENTRY** is the industry model that makes loyalty happen, since its measurements are aligned with consumer value creation. 5. Profit growth will be based on marketing productivity. The opportunity is tremendous. Marketing productivity will in turn drive logistics productivity. If done properly, the industry will approach theoretical optimization through continuous improvement. Failure to change to a marketing productivity model will open the door for outsiders to enter and take advantage of the false economics.	1. Store size will limit growth; in fact, the larger the store, the less it meets the moment of value need. 2. Are you kidding? 3. Size, land-based stores, financial power, logistics capability. 4. Quarterly results. 5. ECR is only focused on the saturated logistics of an old model.
9. Achieve ECR Objectives	1. Compare the ECR objectives of efficient assortments, efficient replentishment, efficient new item introductions and efficient promotions to the **AGENTRY AGENDA**™.	1. I rest my case!

Relevant Research By Andersen Consulting

Grocery Distribution in the 90's: Strategies for Fast Flow Replenishment, Sponsor: The Coca-Cola Retailing Research Group (Europe), May 1992.

Horizon Scan Project, Sponsor: Uniform Code Council, January 1993.

Building Competitive Advantage with GM/HBC, Sponsor: American Greetings Research Council, May 1994.

Wholesale Food Distribution: Today and Tomorrow, Sponsor: National-American Wholesalers Grocers' Association, October 1994.

The Retail Problem of Out-of-Stock Merchandise, Sponsor: The Coca-Cola Retailing Research Council, January 1996.

Supply Meets Demand, Sponsor: U.S. Distribution Journal, January 1996.

Foodservice: Does It Make Cents? Understanding the Economics of Foodservice from a Grocer's Perspective, Sponsor: Food Marketing Institute, March 1996.

Broker 2000: The Role of the Food Broker in the Year 2000 and Beyond, Sponsor: Association Sales & Marketing Companies, December 1996.

Invoice Accuracy: Meeting and Aligning Trading Partner Expectations, Sponsor: Grocery Manufacturers of America, February 1997.

Solution Selling I: Coming Soon to a Store Near You, Sponsor: Grocery Manufacturers of America, April 1997.

Understanding Consumer Direct, Sponsor: Consumer Direct Cooperative, January 1998.

Supply Chain Solutions: Linking the Chains, Sponsor: Food Logistics, March 1998.

The Daunting Dilemma of Trade Promotion, Sponsor: Andersen Consulting, April 1998.

Solution Selling II: Delivering the New Shopping Experience, Sponsor: Grocery Manufacturers of America, June 1998.

Solution Selling III: Total Store Solutions, Sponsor: Grocery Manufacturers of America, April 1999.

To order copies of the research reports please contact the report sponsor.